THE PLACE WE CALL HOME

Books by Robert J. Grant

Love and Roses from David—
A Legacy of Living and Dying (out of print)

Are We Listening to the Angels?

The Place We Call Home—
Exploring the Soul's Existence After Death

THE PLACE WE CALL HOME

EXPLORING THE SOUL'S EXISTENCE AFTER DEATH

by Robert J. Grant

with a Foreword by George G. Ritchie, Jr., M.D.

ARE PRESS

ASSOCIATION FOR
RESEARCH AND
ENLIGHTENMENT

A.R.E. Press • Virginia Beach • Virginia

A.R.E. Press
215 67th Street
Virginia Beach, VA 23451-2061

Grant, Robert J.
    The place we call home : exploring the soul's existence after death / by Robert J. Grant : with a foreword by George Ritchie.—1st ed.
        p.   cm.
    Includes bibliographical references.
    ISBN 0-87604-457-7
    1. Future life. 2. Cayce, Edgar, 1877-1945. Edgar Cayce readings. I. Title.
BF1311.F8 G72   2000
133.9'01'3—dc21   99-27934

    Grateful acknowledgment is made to the following publishers for permission to reprint from their publications:
    Testimony of Light, by Helen Greaves. Reprinted by permission of Neville Spearman Publishers, The C.W. Daniel Company Limited, 1 Church Path, Saffron Walden, Essex CB10 1JP, England. Copyright © 1969 by Helen Greaves.
    The Boy Who Saw True, Anonymous, with Introduction, Afterword, and Notes by Cyril Scott. Reprinted by permission of C.W. Daniel Co., Ltd., Publishers, 1 Church Path, Saffron Walden, Essex CB10 1JP, England. Copyright © 1953 by SL.
    There Is a River—The Story of Edgar Cayce, by Thomas Sugrue. Reprinted by permission of the publisher, A.R.E. Press. Copyright © 1973 by Patricia Sugrue Channon.
    Life, Death and Psychical Research, edited by Canon J. D. Pearce-Higgins and Rev. G. Stanley Whitby. Reprinted by permission of Rider and Company, 3 Fitzroy Square, London W1. Copyright © 1973 by The Churches' Fellowship for Psychical and Spiritual Studies.
    The Tibetan Book of Living and Dying, by Sogyal Rinpoche. Reprinted by permission of HarperCollins Publishers, 10 East 53rd Street, New York, NY 10022. Copyright © 1993 by Rigpa Fellowship.

Cover design by Kim Cohen
Cover art "In the Clear Light," by James Yax, © 1980

For
Lois Irene Bennett
with love

Contents

Acknowledgments

There are many people who contributed in vital ways to this project. First of all, I'd like to thank G. Scott Sparrow, a true friend and inspiring mentor; his life-long spiritual journey has illuminated the pathways of my own and brought me peace and inspiration.

I also must thank George Ritchie, M.D., a true visionary and spiritual pioneer who had the courage to be the first physician to publicly "come out of the closet" to share the story of his near-death experience with medical students, fellow professors, colleagues, and laypeople. Like those of all true visionaries, his stories changed the world, including my own, for the better.

I am deeply grateful to the late Hugh Lynn Cayce. This man took me under his wing when I was barely twenty. He spent many hours helping me overcome fear and understand the continuity of life and the eternal nature of the soul. Little did I know at the time of his mentorship that he was in the final months of his life, battling terminal cancer. The Bible contains a verse that defines the character of the Hugh Lynn I was privileged to know: "Greater love hath no man but that he would give his life for his friends."

Deep gratitude also goes to Michael C. Francis and Clinton Wallace, two friends who were there for me with loads of encouragement and support during the best of times, the worst of times, that this book was in progress.

I send a world of thanks to Sandi Ekberg and family for opening their doors and making me a part of the family during a time of great personal and professional transition.

Special thanks also go to Charles W. Marks, M.D., one of the few physicians I've met who has remembered the spiritual premise of "physician as healer" and has never taken up the more popular credo, "physician as auto mechanic." Thanks Dr. Marks, for keeping me alive, lo, these past three books.

Deep and heartfelt thanks to Stevie Nicks, whose poetic voice helped me find my own as a writer and speaker: "I'll follow you down 'til the sound of my voice will haunt you . . . " Thank you, for that benevolent haunting.

Thanks to my wonderful family for their understanding, support, and love throughout the years—my parents George and Mary Lou Grant, and my brothers John and Jim Grant.

I am deeply grateful to Steve and Gail Daily, Fred and Evelyn Billingsley, Jim Williams, Jan and Rick Hunter, Heather Drake, and Ron and Marguerite Nelson, for giving me a great deal of material and spiritual support.

Special thanks to my talented editors Joseph Dunn and Brenda English.

Last but not least, this book would not have been possible were it not for the amazing people who patiently provided many interview hours and answered scores of questions about their illuminating life and near-death experiences that are contained within these pages. Thank you, and God bless each of you.

Foreword

I consider it a high honor that Rob Grant has called on me to write the foreword for this book.

Almost three years ago, I was in Fort Lauderdale, Florida, speaking—with Rob—to the A.R.E. chapter of that fine city. I was deeply impressed, not only with this young man's delivery, but also with his profound insight into the material which came through the Edgar Cayce readings. Since then, I have been with Rob on at least two more occasions, in California and New York City.

During these meetings, I have had the opportunity to come to know Rob in a deeper way, which answered the question that came into my mind when I first heard him speak: How did such a young person have the spiritual and intellectual capacity to adequately read and gain such a clear insight into what was coming through Edgar Cayce?

During the almost three years that have followed, I have learned about the psychological trauma through which Rob passed during his teenage years. I recognized something that I have learned from forty years as a youth leader, thirteen years as a family physician, and twenty-four years as a psychiatrist: Heartaches, disillusionments, disappointments, and hurts from people you least expect will either cause a soul to become bitter, hostile, angry, and disillusioned in life or drive the soul to search above and beyond just the physical and material things of life into a quest for spiritual things and into the arms of God. This latter is what happened to Rob and prepared him to be ready when he came under the watchful care of Hugh Lynn Cayce. He had already developed a deeper understanding of spiritual and mental things than most people twice his age.

This background, along with his years with Hugh Lynn Cayce and the A.R.E., has enabled Rob to write this book, which is a compilation of experiences of people like Edgar Cayce and others who have informed us about life on the other side of what we call death.

These people have brought back to us what life is all about after we die. Rob has demonstrated the ability to communicate in the most clear and concise way what they have been trying to tell us. I say this, for he has taken my own experience and the implications of this experience and made them clearer than I feel even I have been able to do. I feel he has also done this with the other people he includes in this book.

As a result, he has written a book that I believe every minister, priest, rabbi, pastor, and youth leader should read. On one side, it removes the fear of death and shows us a God of the most profound love we have ever known or can ever experience. On the other side, Rob clearly brings to us—from all these people's experiences—the message that it is not a God of love, like the Christ, who sends bad things upon us, but our own actions which can and will bring disaster upon us and the ones we love.

We learn from reading this book that the pathways we take on this side of death determine the path we will walk on the other side.

After reading this book, you will never again believe that we have no knowledge of life after death. This is the handbook we need to help us prepare for the realms to come.

George G. Ritchie, Jr., M.D.
Professor of Psychiatry,
University of Virginia (retired)
Author of *Return from Tomorrow*

"For life and death are one,
even as the river and the sea are one."
—Khalil Gibran

Preface

*I*n December 1944, Edgar Cayce lay dying in his Virginia Beach home. Three strokes in the preceding months had left him partially paralyzed and unable to speak above a whisper. Suffering from an array of illnesses, Cayce also had pulmonary edema which made it impossible for him to lie prone. He could sleep only by sitting in a chair or propped in the hospital bed. If he lay prone, Cayce would strangle to death and drown from the fluid in his lungs.

Exhausted and gaunt, unable to rest, eat, or walk, Cayce looked far older than his sixty-seven years. Those close to Edgar Cayce at the time of his terminal illness agreed that the most tragic aspect wasn't his critical state of physical health, but his inconsolable mental depression.

Edgar Cayce was convinced that his life and work were

failures. Neither his wife, Gertrude, nor his closest associate and secretary, Gladys Davis, could dispel the depression that haunted his mind like dark shadows, always repeating the same thing: "You did this to yourself, Edgar. You knew how to take care of yourself, Edgar, and you didn't. You ruined your own health; you are abandoning the people who need you."

Edgar Cayce had been psychically gifted all his life, and he gave readings every day for people who needed medical, emotional, and spiritual help. He had always made himself available for anyone who asked for a reading. In his final months, it was his own abilities that had deteriorated his health. The requests for his psychic readings came in by the hundreds as a result of the national publication of his biography, *There Is a River—The Story of Edgar Cayce*, by Thomas Sugrue. It was irony at its finest: Edgar Cayce had endured much criticism and public disbelief because of his psychic gifts. Once his biography received stellar reviews in the *Boston Globe*, the *New York Tribune*, and other publications, Cayce finally was embraced by the masses. His life and work, so very difficult to explain to even the most open-minded people, were validated. *He was validated.* Prior to the publication of his biography, much of the outside world consistently denounced him as a fraud. Yet, Thomas Sugrue, Cayce's biographer, owed his life to his book's subject, and his testimony of life with Cayce was the stuff of which miracles are made. Sugrue was a paralyzed cripple when he came to Cayce's home. Two years later, he was walking again after physicians had said there was no hope of such a thing. More, Sugrue went on to write more books beyond *River*, after Edgar Cayce's untimely death. The physicians who denounced Cayce also denounced any idea that Sugrue could walk again. And yet, he did.

Because the demand for Cayce's readings became so

great, he pushed himself to the limit giving sometimes eight to ten readings per day even after he was told, in his own readings, not to give more than two per day at the risk of his physical health. Cayce could not, would not turn anyone away, and he told Gertrude, who pleaded with her husband to slow down, "I've got to do it until I can't do it anymore. Too many people need help." So, Edgar Cayce continued the accelerated pace of the readings, knowing that by doing so he was risking his life.

During his lifetime, Edgar Cayce's psychic abilities provided hope to thousands who had been hopeless. His ability to accurately diagnose illness in people he had never seen and to prescribe medical treatments unknown to his conscious mind had saved Gertrude from an early death from tuberculosis. His older son, Hugh Lynn, was spared a life of blindness when an explosion damaged his eyes so severely that physicians said the boy would never see again. And a woman who was utterly paralyzed from infantile paralysis walked—when physicians had said the woman would be bedridden.

As he lay dying, Edgar Cayce could not rest because he knew so many more people needed help, even though he no longer was physically or psychically able to help them. Cayce did not realize that the many thousands of readings he *had* given would live on and inspire scientists, physicians, and lay people long after his death. He did not realize during his final hours that, through him, a biblical prophecy had come to pass, thanks to his psychic gift: "The lame shall walk, the blind shall receive their sight, and the deaf shall hear."

I did not know Edgar Cayce during his lifetime, but as a student of his readings for more than twenty years, I feel I know him intimately. I was privileged to spend five years with the team that computerized the 14,305 psychic readings Edgar Cayce left behind. This book is the result of the important guidance I received through his readings. Just as Cayce was a beacon of light to thousands who were in physical, mental, and spiritual need, he was also a light to me in helping me understand the transition we call death. Death, Cayce said, is nothing more than passing through "God's other door," where life continues, relationships are renewed, and the soul lives on in realms beyond our physical vision, but in worlds in some ways not too far different from this one. During my spiritual search, Cayce's readings on life after death represented an oasis of illuminating knowledge that quelled my fears, gave me peace, and answered many questions I had about the mysterious journey we call death. My questions, I realize, were not unique; they have been asked for eons by every person who ever walked the earth: Where do we go when we die? Is there a heaven? Is there hell? Do we gather with our loved ones after death, or are they gone from us forever? Does *any* part of me survive after death? If so, what part of me survives? Where are all the people I've known and loved who have died? Do they still know and love me? Can I still communicate with them?

These questions became of paramount importance to me relatively early in my life. I came under the guidance of a fundamentalist Christian minister who took it upon himself to teach me about eternal damnation, the fiery torments of hell, and the perilous state of my soul (I was twelve or thirteen years old at the time). Up to that point in my life, I had never had reason to disbelieve what adults told me. I was raised in a very open-minded and loving home, and such dark subjects that the minister introduced me to had never surfaced. What frightened me the worst was his assertion that most people were going straight to hell after physical death—forever. Only a few would be "saved." Twelve- and thirteen-year-old boys are impressionable creatures. The impressions the minister made upon my mind were deep, and I was filled with a marked sense of fear and dread when I thought about life after death. I experienced many nightmares and unsettling dreams. As I look back upon those experiences, I realize that I had been mentally traumatized by the minister. Yet, paradoxically, the fear that that was instilled was the force that propelled me to begin my spiritual search for answers about the nature of life, death, and the soul. I became obsessed with learning as much as I could about the "unseen worlds." My mother was a voracious reader, and she passed on her love of books to me. Naturally, I devoured books from many different spiritual philosophies and traditions. At one point, my father suggested that if I was going to read books on psychic sciences or spirituality, I would do well to read up on Edgar Cayce. His advice was a much-needed answer to a prayer. In Cayce's readings, I was relieved to find that my fears about what lies beyond "God's other door" were unfounded. I found in Cayce's readings a practical philosophy for spiritual living that considers life here in this world and the life after death as *one*.

It is my hope that this book will in some way help others attain a sense of peace and understanding about the nature of death. I also hope that this book will help readers move beyond grief into healing, and out of the shadows of fear into a place of light and reassurance. I feel a great sense of privilege to have come to know the legacy of Edgar Cayce, for I am more than assured and have faith that he was indeed right: Life *is* a continuous experience, and we are as eternal as the Source Who lovingly brought us into being.

Robert J. Grant
Norfolk, Virginia
June 1999

1

Edgar Cayce: Discovering the Unseen Worlds

"Everybody has psychic ability, just as everybody has the ability to strike the keys of a piano keyboard. But, of course, not everybody develops these abilities to the level of becoming a concert pianist."
—Arthur Ford

Since time immemorial, in every culture throughout the world and in every age, there have always been people who were gifted with second sight—the sixth sense—powers of perception beyond the range of the five senses. They have been called various names in different periods of history: soothsayers, saints, prophets, sages, seers, psychics, mediums, spiritualists, channelers. These people sometimes seem to inhabit a world apart from their friends and families, who perceive the world and universe solely through five senses. The seers inexplicably possess the sixth sense, which enables them to see "through the veil" of the material world, connect with the spiritual realms, and communicate with the souls who reside there.

Going to a psychic or medium for a reading has gained widespread acceptance only in recent years. Before psychics and psychic readings were reported by the mass media, an excursion to see a psychic or a medium was considered very controversial and usually was kept very quiet. But almost everyone can recall a coincidental experience, a dream, or vision that had an otherworldly or psychic quality to it. Psychic ability represents the senses of the soul. There are facets of our life experiences that cannot be understood from the three-dimensional standpoint. The intangible nature of the soul or spirit, as well as our thought processes and feelings, all are evidence that there is a greater, unseen reality permeating our material world as well as our inner lives.

Frequently, people will seek the guidance of a psychic during a crisis—for which no answers can be found in the material world; such is often the "breakthrough" point where we seek answers from the spiritual realm. For instance, the grief that accompanies the unexpected death of a loved one frequently will prompt a person to seek psychic guidance and spiritual counsel. In the mid- to late 1800s, large numbers of people in England and the United States began attending séances and visiting mediums, in hopes of communicating with their deceased friends or family members. Such communications offered a unique opportunity to transcend the material world and experience life beyond the confines of the physical world. Scores of people have found a great deal of comfort and reassurance and been able to let go of their grief after going to a gifted seer. In the last half century, a few gifted psychics and mediums rose to the national spotlight because of their ability to communicate with souls who exist in unseen realms: Arthur Ford, Jane Roberts, Ruth Montgomery, Eileen Garrett. Today, more credibility and acceptance are being given to psychic phenomena and to individual psychics.

One man who barely had an eighth-grade education helped pave the way, through his psychic gift, for understanding the unseen link between the material and the spiritual worlds. His name was Edgar Cayce, and in the early part of the twentieth century, he began a pioneering journey that would eventually lead him to become known as the most documented psychic in the world. Cayce possessed a great many psychic gifts and abilities: He was telepathic, clairvoyant, clairaudient, had the ability to be a medium, and was precognitive in the waking as well as the trance state.

Edgar Cayce was telepathic and clairvoyant both awake and unconscious. To him, there was no real difference between the material and spiritual worlds; all of his life he had the ability to see through the veil and communicate with the dead. The Cayce family took special care to document and preserve the records of his conscious psychic experiences along with the more than 14,000 "readings" he left behind at his death in 1945. Edgar Cayce was very much a man who walked between two worlds. His readings about life in the unseen realms and descriptions of the various planes the soul travels to after physical death represent one of the most cohesive descriptions ever recorded about the soul's existence outside the boundaries of the material world.

Cayce's psychic abilities manifested when he was just a little boy. He told his mother and grandmother that he frequently saw and talked with his deceased grandfather, whom he loved dearly. Instead of dismissing him for having an overactive imagination, Edgar's mother and grandmother listened intently to Edgar's stories about his encounters with his dead grandfather, and they believed him.

It might seem strange that two rural farm women living in Christian County, Kentucky, would be knowledgeable about such things, but psychic ability was very much a part of the Cayce family. Edgar's grandfather, Thomas Jefferson Cayce, had psychic abilities all of his life. He was a well-known dowser or "well witcher" in Christian County, and the farmers came from near and far to hire the elder Cayce to help them find water. He demonstrated other psychic abilities as well.

"Your grandfather was a remarkable man," Grandmother Cayce said. "Anything he touched would grow. He had more than a green thumb; it was like magic. All the wells in this neighborhood were dug where he told the men to dig them, and they always found water. Many's the day a neighbor would come and ask him to locate a well. Off he'd go, and somewhere along the way he'd cut a hazel twig, with a good fork. Then he'd walk around the ground on which the farmer wanted the well, until the twig told him where to stop. The little branches on the fork of the twig would twitch. 'Right here,' he'd say, and there they'd dig and there they'd find water.

"He could make tables and chairs move," she added, "and brooms dance without touching them. I don't believe anyone ever saw him do it but myself. He used to say to me, 'Everything comes from God . . . The Lord said there is set before each of us good and evil, for us to choose. So if I spend all my time making brooms dance and doing tricks for people's entertainment, that would be choosing evil.'"[1]

Grandmother Cayce instilled the same principle in her grandson. She instructed Edgar very early on to read the Bible and to ask, in his daily prayers, for guidance and direction on how to use his spiritual gifts. Edgar followed her advice in earnest, and it wasn't long before he began to have mystical experiences.

"As a child, I prayed that I might be able to do something for the other fellow," Cayce said, "to aid others in understanding themselves, and especially to aid children in their ills. I had a vision one day which convinced me that my prayer had been heard and would be answered."[2]

While reading the Bible in his favorite spot in the woods, the young Cayce suddenly became aware of a beautiful woman standing before him. He was filled with awe and amazement as this woman was not from this world: he could see the outline of wings. The woman then told Edgar that she had come to grant him a wish. After he told the woman he wanted to be helpful to others, particularly children, she vanished as quickly as she had appeared. Edgar Cayce didn't know it at the time, but his wish would be fulfilled in ways he never could have imagined during his lifetime. The uplifting vision that Edgar experienced was the first of many that he would have as a child in his favorite spot in the woods. He wrote about that place and his early psychic experiences to a friend many years later:

> . . . when I had grown to be six or seven years old our home was in a little wood . . . we lived there for several years. It was there that I read the Bible through the first time, that I learned to pray, that I had many visions or experiences . . . what seemed to me to be the hosts that must have appeared to the people of old . . . 464-12, Reports

When Edgar Cayce was twenty-four, he lost his voice. It dwindled gradually, painlessly, to a bare whisper. The laryngitis remained for almost two years. Specialists were called in from all parts of Kentucky, yet they could find nothing physically wrong with Cayce's vocal chords. Finally, a rather unorthodox hypnotist named Al C. Layne heard about the mysterious malady and offered to try to help Cayce. After placing him under hypnosis, Layne suggested to Cayce's subconscious mind that he would be able to speak normally. While in the hypnotic trance, Cayce spoke clearly for the first time in nearly two years, although his speech had a strange monotone quality to it. Cayce spoke as if he were observing himself from a distance and referred to himself in the third person. While in trance, Cayce diagnosed his own medical condition, saying it was brought on by impaired circulation and stress. After a pause, Cayce instructed the hypnotist to repeat a suggestion that the circulation was completely normal. Layne followed the suggestion and then brought Cayce out of the hypnotic trance. When Cayce came back to waking consciousness moments later, his voice was completely restored. Everyone—including Cayce—was astonished. While he was delighted to have his voice back, he was also startled: Cayce had no conscious recall of anything he had said while under hypnosis.

Years later, Cayce recounted those early days at a lecture: "The gentleman who assisted in this first reading believed that if I could describe what was wrong with myself I might also help others. He asked me to try so I began spending much of my time in an unconscious state giving information for those who, hearing of this unusual power, sought help."[3]

Eventually, he learned to put himself in the trance state without the help of a hypnotist and had a stenographer write down every word of his unconscious dissertations. After a time, it was discovered that Cayce needed only the name and address of the person seeking help;

the person didn't have to be present in the room for the reading, nor did Cayce require any background information on the person prior to the psychic reading. The accuracy of his medical diagnoses was consistently high, there didn't seem to be a limit to the information Cayce had access to while in the unconscious state. It seemed that the hope of Cayce's grandmother and mother was fulfilled—Edgar Cayce indeed had second sight. His gift helped thousands of people find relief from their physical illnesses and thousands more find greater meaning and purpose to their lives through his spiritual readings. Yet Cayce never took the credit himself when the readings proved accurate and helpful for people. He was rather shy about discussing his psychic abilities; he held sacred the gift that had been given to him, and he remained humble throughout his life.

A parade of mediums, psychics, and stargazers have marched across the world's stage over the last century; many yearned for the spotlight, notoriety, and celebrity. Edgar Cayce shied away from publicity to the extent that not a single photograph appears to exist of his giving a reading. He never sought fame nor did he boast about his abilities. In the early years of his psychic work, Cayce rarely discussed the readings with "outsiders."

"I was . . . ashamed to talk about these readings," Cayce wrote. "People thought me odd and I resented for a time the little slights and slurs of my associates who took pleasure in laughing at me. It is hard to be 'different.' I finally selected photography as a life work and gave only my spare time and evenings to the increasing number of requests for readings. It was only when I began to come in contact with those who received help from following the suggestions given in readings that I began to realize the true nature of the work which lay before me . . . "[4]

Author Thomas Sugrue, lifelong friend of the Cayce
family and Edgar Cayce's biographer, poetically wrote of
Cayce's struggle to accept his unusual powers:

> To convince himself that he was not a freak of
> nature, not an unconscious fraud, not a spiritual
> charlatan, was first of all the work of Edgar Cayce.
> For years he lived in self-conscious embarrassment
> because of his strange peculiarity, for years he
> feared to give the aid requested of him because he
> did not know nor understand the thing he did. For
> years his life was a mental torture, a seething inde-
> cision, a labyrinth of ideas, ideals, misbeliefs and
> disillusions . . .
> He survived the cries that branded him charla-
> tan, quack, spiritualist, clairvoyant, hypnotist, fake
> and fraud. He survived the misunderstanding, pain,
> disillusionment, loss of friends and attacks of en-
> emies. He survived the purgatory of ignorance . . .
> finding peace and happiness in the knowledge of
> truth and the possession of an ideal.[5]

It was found that Cayce could answer any question on
any subject posed to him while in the unconscious state.
The range of his psychic vision while asleep seemed to
be unlimited; he seemed able to access an infinite reservoir of physical, mental, and spiritual knowledge. From
this reservoir, Cayce drew from many sources to obtain
the information requested. The following extract is from
one of Cayce's readings that describes how and where he
was able to retrieve information while in the trance state:

> The information obtained and given by this body
> is obtained through the power of mind over mind
> . . . It obtains its information . . . either from other

subconscious minds—put in touch with the power of . . . suggestion . . . or from minds that have passed into the Beyond . . . What is known to one subconscious mind or soul is known to another, whether conscious of the fact or not . . . 254-2

The "power of suggestion" mentioned above was the hypnotic suggestion that was read aloud by the "conductor" as Edgar Cayce entered the sleep state. This suggestion determined the type of information Cayce would obtain for the individual who requested the reading (medical, mental-spiritual, dream interpretation, etc.). Cayce's subconscious mind followed the directions given in the suggestion *to the letter.* If the suggestion was vague or general, usually the information which came through was of a general nature. A concisely-worded, specific suggestion enabled Cayce to provide information in greater detail and clarity. In another reading, Cayce said:

. . . the body, Edgar Cayce, in the psychic or subconscious condition, is able . . . to reach all the subconscious minds, when directed to such subconscious minds by suggestion, whether in the material world or in the spiritual world . . . Edgar Cayce, in the subconscious condition, may communicate with those passed into the spiritual plane. 900-22

In other words, a part of Cayce's subconscious mind traveled through time and space and retrieved information from the minds of other people in the earth and from those who had passed on. When this facet of his psychic work became more well known, many people came to Edgar Cayce to ask questions about the deeper meaning of life and the mysteries of death. One of the

most frequently asked questions on this subject concerned what happens to the soul after death. Those who
sought answers did not leave empty-handed. Cayce's
unconscious detailed a road map for death—once called
the mysterious journey from which no traveler returns
to tell the tale. According to the readings, the soul's final
journey from this world is as natural as being born into
it. Many people came to ask Cayce about their deceased
friends and loved ones. Not a few of them came in hopes
of receiving a message from the other side. Cayce was not a
medium, in the classic sense, but there were occasions
when he relayed messages from the deceased person to
the one who requested the reading. On rare occasions,
the deceased spoke directly through Cayce and gave a
message to the seeker. Edgar Cayce detailed his thoughts
and feelings about this subject at one of his lectures:

> Some people think that the information coming
> through me is given by some departed personality
> who wants to communicate with them, or some
> benevolent spirit or physician from the other side.
> This may sometimes be the case though in general
> I am not a 'medium' in that sense of the term. How-
> ever, if a person comes seeking that kind of contact
> and information, I believe he receives it . . . If an
> individual's desire is very intense to have a commu-
> nication from Grandpa, Uncle, or some great soul,
> the contact is directed that way, and that becomes
> the source [of the psychic information]. Do not
> think that I am discrediting those who seek in that
> way. If you're willing to receive what Uncle Joe has
> to say, that's what you get; if you're willing to depend
> on a more universal source, that's what you get.[6]

Hugh Lynn Cayce was a lifelong researcher, student,

and teacher of the topics in his father's readings. He offered the following insights on the "mechanics" of how Cayce's clairvoyant abilities worked and how information was obtained:

> Edgar Cayce said he could withdraw from the physical body just as one withdraws at death. Because of his development, he was then free to move through many levels of consciousness. He could also attune to higher levels of consciousness, to touch the aspirations, purposes and development of the soul-mind . . . He could tune in to thought-patterns and thought-forms . . . In addition, he could tune in to the minds of entities on various planes other than the earth.[7]

Edgar Cayce's childhood ability to see and communicate with his deceased grandfather stayed with him throughout his lifetime, and he had many fascinating encounters with a variety of people who were in various planes of consciousness in the afterlife. In one lecture, Cayce discussed the following story to emphasize that there was no real difference between the worlds of the living and the dead. This experience happened to him while he was traveling on a train:

> A young man came in the smoking room, sat down by my side, and struck up a conversation: "Well I have just come to. I was drowned day before yesterday at Virginia Beach. My brother was not revived and is being taken home in his coffin on this same train." I would like to try to convey to you [the survivor's] experience just as he told it to me. He knew he was going. He felt his strength give out. As he sank exhausted into the waters, he realized that

it was the bluest water he had ever seen—everything was very, very blue. Yet strangely enough he was happy ... He was with his mother, even though he knew perfectly well she wasn't in the water because she had been buried back in Kentucky. But he was very conscious of her presence, and she was urging him to make at least one more effort. He was not conscious after that of feeling any fear or making any more effort. He was not even conscious of being taken out of the water, or of anything that happened after he was taken out of the water. But what was most interesting to me ... as he expressed it, there is no difference between the living physical experience and the unseen experience, except that the unseen world—to us—is not as populated as the seen world. When death comes to an individual he knows he has passed from what we call life into what we call death. There's no fear in death if there is no fear in life.[8]

On several occasions, just before he entered the unconscious trance state to give a reading, Cayce experienced other dimensions of life that exist after physical death. Cayce said this experience was the best illustration to him, of some of the places the soul may find itself after physical death:

On going into the unconscious state [to obtain a psychic reading], I recognized that I was leaving my body. There was just a direct, straight, and narrow line in front of me, like a shaft of white light. On either side was fog and smoke and many shadowy figures who seemed to be crying to me for help, and begging me to come aside to the state they occupied. As I followed along the shaft of light, the way began to clear. The figures on either side grew more distinct; they took on clearer form. But [they seemed to be] attempting to sidetrack me and bring me aside from my purpose. Yet with the narrow way in front of me I kept going straight ahead. After a bit I passed to where the figures were merely shadows attempting to assist; they urged me on rather than attempted to stop me. Then they took on form, and they seemed to be occupied with their own activities. When they paid any attention to me at all it was rather to urge me on. Finally, I came to a hill, where there was a mount and a temple. I entered this temple and found in it a very large room, very much like a library. They were the books of people's lives, for each person's activities were a matter of actual record, it seemed, and I merely had to pull down the record of the individual for whom I was seeking information. That was [my] actual experience.[9]

Edgar Cayce believed this experience was very real. He had a heightened state of awareness as he passed through the dimensions; he believed that the realms he passed through to obtain the psychic information were the same realms through which the soul passes after physical death. Certain elements were disconcerting to him. For instance, the shadow figures who were crying out for help represented to him those souls who were "earthbound." Cayce's readings indicated that human desires and attachments to the earth don't simply "die" upon physical death. Desires, passions, and habits that the mind has cultivated during physical life are not left behind when the soul departs the body. These invisible desires of the inner self go with the soul when it passes out of the physical body at death. If these earthly desires are powerful enough, they create a world where the soul lives in the shadows of its earthly desires, longings, and thoughts. This self-created world can hold the soul in an earthbound state, inhibiting its ability to grow beyond what Cayce called "earth-earthy" awareness. On the other hand, if a person's desires have been so spiritualized that they are free from earthly attachments, desires, and concerns, the soul will awaken in a light-filled realm where they experience great joy, peace, and contentment. Cayce said during a lecture:

When a soul passes from the physical body, it continues to build . . . As we live day by day, as we apply the abilities and talents that we have, we shall have with us after the transition called death exactly those soul qualities that we have acquired on earth. When we pass over our experience will not be very different from passing from one room to another; for "In my Father's house are many mansions . . . " It is up to us as to how we furnish our room in that other mansion. If we furnish it with beauty, then that will be our first experience on awakening in the shadow-land. If ours has been a life of malice, selfishness, and hate, then those things must be met in exactly the form we have built them, either in this life or the next. If it has been a life of love, a life of self-sacrifice for another, then love will be our reward as we enter into the other experience.[10]

2

Images of Life After Dying:
Near-Death Experiences

For life and death are one, and only those who will consider the experience as one may come to understand or comprehend what peace indeed means.   Edgar Cayce Reading 1977-1

*I*n 1932, Edgar Cayce predicted that one day the mystery of death would be unraveled, and humanity would gain a true understanding that physical death is only a transition from one level of experience to another:

(Q) What is the significance of the empty Sarcophagus [in the Great Pyramid]?
(A) That there will be no more death. Don't misunderstand or misinterpret! but the *interpretation* of death will be made plain. 5748-6

This prophecy appeared to be fulfilled when reports
of a phenomenon called near-death experiences or
NDEs came to light in recent years. George Ritchie, M.D.,
a professor of psychiatry at the University of Virginia,
once told the story of his nine-minute near-death experience to the students in one of his psychology courses.
One of the graduate students attending Dr. Ritchie's lecture was Raymond A. Moody, now a psychiatrist and
best-selling author. Dr. Moody explained:

> I was twenty-one years old at the time in 1965
> when I heard Dr. Ritchie tell this phenomenal story.
> Up to that time, I didn't believe anything happened
> after death. I hadn't had any experience that led me
> to believe there was anything after this life. I was an
> atheist in the sense that I never believed in the pun-
> ishing, judgmental God that the Christian funda-
> mentalists believed in. As far as I was concerned,
> when you're dead, that was the end of it. Dr. Ritchie's
> account of the afterlife impressed me a great deal—
> but I didn't actively research the phenomena until
> several years later.[1]

A major turning point occurred when Dr. Moody was
an associate professor of philosophy at West Georgia
State College. Dr. Moody was teaching a course on tha-
natology, the study of death and dying, when one of his
students asked a provocative question:

> He wanted to know if I was going to discuss life
> after death during the course of the class. I noticed
> that he looked like he had been through a traumatic
> accident of some sort—he had numerous scars on
> his body. When I asked him what prompted such a
> question, he said, "Because I had an accident and a

very strange experience." When I asked him to elaborate, he started telling me the identical story I'd heard George Ritchie tell me years earlier at UVA about his experiences after clinical death. I was absolutely astonished![2]

Dr. Moody was so intrigued by the commonalties between Ritchie's experience and his student's that he decided to study the phenomenon in depth. He attended medical school and spent many hours interviewing patients who were pronounced dead and then resuscitated. Dr. Moody published his research in the book, *Life After Life*, and offered the following synopsis of the common elements inherent in a near-death experience:

A man is dying and, as he reaches the point of greatest physical distress, he hears himself pronounced dead by his doctor. He begins to hear an uncomfortable noise, a loud ringing or buzzing, and at the same time feels himself moving very rapidly through a long dark tunnel. After this, he suddenly finds himself outside of his own physical body, but still in the immediate physical environment, and he sees his own body from a distance, as though he is a spectator. He watches the resuscitation attempt from this unusual vantage point ... He notices that he still has a "body," but one of a very different nature and with very different powers from the physical body he has left behind. Soon other things begin to happen. Others come to meet and to help him. He glimpses the spirits of relatives and friends who have already died, and a loving, warm spirit of a kind he has never encountered before—a being of light—appears before him. This being asks him a question, nonverbally, to make

him evaluate his life and helps him along by showing him a panoramic, instantaneous playback of
the major events of his life . . . [Then] he finds that
he must go back to earth, that the time for his death
has not yet come. At this point he resists, for by now
he is taken up with his experiences in the afterlife
and does not want to return. He is overwhelmed by
intense feelings of joy, love, and peace. Despite his
attitude, though, he somehow reunites with his
body and lives. Later he tries to tell others, but he
has trouble doing so. In the first place, he can find
no human words adequate to describe these un-
earthly episodes. He also finds that others scoff, so
he stops telling other people. Still, the experience
affects his life profoundly, especially his views
about death and its relationship to life.[3]

Dr. Moody's book has given the world a clear picture
of the first stage of life after the threshold of physical
death, and his findings seemed to be a fulfillment of
Cayce's prediction that "the *interpretation* of death will
be made plain."

One of the earliest written accounts of the near-death
experience dates back to the year 1893. Dr. Thomson Jay
Hudson, a philosopher and theologian, wrote an account in his book, *The Law of Psychic Phenomena*, that
bears a striking resemblance to Dr. Moody's reports of
the near-death phenomenon:

A lady who is now at the head of one of the largest orphan asylums of a Western city has been twice
pronounced dead by the attending physicians,
twice prepared for the grave, and twice resuscitated
by her friends. On the last occasion extraordinary
precautions were taken, in view of her former expe-

rience. All the tests known to her physicians were applied, and all doubts were set at rest. She was a second time professionally declared to be dead, and the physicians left the house. In preparing the body for burial [she] was accidentally pricked by a pin. Soon afterwards it was discovered that a small drop of blood marked the spot where the pin entered . . . vigorous treatment soon restored her to consciousness. She is living today, a vigorous useful woman. It is proper to note here that upon being restored, the lady declared that she had never for a moment lost consciousness, that she knew all that went on around her, perfectly comprehended the significance of all the tests which were applied, but felt the utmost indifference as to the result, and was neither surprised nor alarmed when it was decided that she was dead.[4]

Since Dr. Moody first began his research, he has collected 30,000 accounts of near-death experiences from around the world. The common thread that runs through these accounts is that each individual came face to face with a Being who conveys complete and unconditional love. They knew without question that the love was an eternal force and would never waver regardless of what the person had done or left undone.

Dr. George Ritchie said this all-powerful love was the most transformational facet of his near-death experience. Fifty-five years since Ritchie had his experience, tears well up in his eyes as he remembers the day he died and met Christ, "the Being who loved every unlovable thing about me."[5]

Dr. Ritchie died from pneumonia and was pronounced dead in a Texas hospital when he was twenty-years old. He "woke up" in the darkened hospital room and was momentarily disoriented. He wandered the halls of the hospital, confused because no one seemed to be able to see or hear him. At that point, he didn't realize he was dead. The full realization didn't dawn on Dr. Ritchie until he wandered back into the hospital room and looked at his bed. He saw a body covered with a sheet, and only a hand of the inert form underneath was visible. With a mixture of confusion and horror, Dr. Ritchie recognized his fraternity ring on the hand:

> There on the left ring finger was my Phi Gamma Delta and University of Richmond ring with 19 on one side and 45 on the other side . . . I could not believe this had happened to me. I was supposed to become the outstanding young doctor! I was going to have a wonderful Christmas with my family . . . Now I would not be able to see any of them again . . . I have never felt so alone, discouraged and frightened.[6]

Dr. Ritchie found himself in a precarious state. He tried without success to reenter his body. He tried to pull the sheet off the body, and his hand went right through it. Dr. Ritchie wondered what to do, where to go:

> Death is instantaneous. One minute you are with your physical body, the next minute you are out of it. You can see that old body, but you are no longer a part of it. It's dead, but believe you me, you're not. To see this corpse lying there in the bed—to realize that I wasn't in any heaven nor hell—to realize I couldn't contact my fellow human beings. I was in a total state of isolation. It was horrible.[7]

At the moment of his greatest distress, the room began to fill with light. Dr. Ritchie initially thought that the dim hospital light was getting brighter at the head of the bed. The light continued to grow in intensity until it was so bright it was almost beyond description.

"If you were to turn on a million welding lights you'd have some idea of the intensity of the light I was seeing," Dr. Ritchie said.[8]

Immediately following the arrival of this light, something deep inside Ritchie's spiritual body spoke to him in the most powerful voice he has ever heard.

"STAND UP," the voice said. "YOU ARE IN THE PRESENCE OF THE SON OF GOD."

"Out of that brilliant light stepped the most amazing being I have ever seen," Dr. Ritchie said. "The hospital walls totally disappeared, I saw . . . every minute detail of my life from the time I was born through my twentieth year . . . With *no detail* left out. How would you like your spouse, your parents, your sisters, brothers, best friend, to know every single thing you had done from the time you were born? That begins to tell the story of how sobering and powerful this experience was."[9]

The life review is an integral part of the near-death experience. Raymond Moody said that the majority of accounts he has collected contains a life review. In panoramic form, every thought, deed, and event are simultaneously replayed and relived. Unlike the traditional Christian belief of Judgment Day when souls will stand before a panel of judgmental beings to determine their eternal abode in heaven or hell, Dr. Moody's near-death experiencers say the soul *judges itself* and the spiritual lessons it learned.

Edgar Cayce once gave a reading for a dying man and said that, at the time of the reading, the man actually was in the final stages of dying and was going through his life review:

Yes, we have the body; and the soul would take leave of same. There are many experiences in a life's journey in the earth that are much more serious than that man calls death . . . For the time [comes], as it must to this body, when no work is to be done but *ye must stand before the judgment bar of thine own conscience* [author's italics], as must each soul, and determine as to whether in the light of the knowledge, in the light of thine opportunity, ye can as thy friend, thy God say, "I have dishonored no man. I have taken naught from my brother, but what I restored fourfold . . . " *For he has been and is viewing those past opportunities that soon shall come no more in this life* . . . [author's italics] 5195-1

"Every detail of twenty years of living was there to be looked at," Dr. Ritchie said. "The good, the bad, the high points, the run-of-the-mill. And with this all-inclusive view came a question. It was implicit in every scene . . . and seemed to proceed from the living Light beside me. *'What did you do with your life?'* It seemed to be a question about values, not facts . . . The question had to do with love: 'How much have you loved with your life? Have you loved others as I am loving you? Totally? Unconditionally?'"[10]

The life review enables the soul to understand completely how it impacted every person it contacted during material life. Souls will realize without a doubt how much they learned how to love, and they will see the instances where they fell short of that ideal. Dr. Ritchie said, however, that *what we think and intend* are as important in the life review as our deeds. As Dr. Ritchie explained, "In the review of my life, I saw my thoughts and intentions as clearly as I saw my deeds. The Being beside me was vitally interested in what I *meant to do.* And believe me, what you mean, what you intend, inside, is a *deed; it is a thing.*"[11]

It's a common experience to have good intentions to help someone and the exact opposite occurs. Nearly everyone can remember a time when he or she meant to help and the gesture was misunderstood, misconstrued, or resulted in turmoil and confusion rather than harmony. Dr. Ritchie said that within the framework of his life review, *his good intentions illuminated the whole of his life.* The things which were of paramount importance, to himself and to Jesus, were the moments in his life when he acted from a spirit of love and compassion. The end result, whether good or bad, was not as important as the intention itself:

> You will see the good you intended—from your heart—in all its glory. And, in my experience with the Risen Christ, He was as overjoyed as I was to see the good I had done. Because the whole purpose was to show me where I'd learned to love as Jesus taught us; and where I fell short. All the while the love never wavered; it never moved.[12]

At long last and once and for all, we banish the axiom "*The road to hell is paved with good intentions.*"

The life review is for the sole benefit of the person who has died—but in the majority of near-death experiences that contain a life review, a spirit guide or light being is present during the review. People of different religious faiths (and those of no particular religious orientation) identify their guide in different ways. In Ritchie's experience, there was no question in his mind that the guide through his near-death experience was Jesus:

> He was totally unlike the pictures I had seen in

the stained glass windows in our churches in Richmond, Virginia. They painted Jesus as a rather nice being—rather thin, rather weak looking. Just before I retired from medicine, I was working out at the Nautilus gym and had a friend who could bench-press 400 pounds. The shoulders on this friend weren't as big as the shoulders on the Being I was standing in front of. Totally different from the Jewish Jesus I had been taught He looked like. Standing in front of him, I could well understand why he could walk through a mob and nobody dared lift a fist. He was not the type of guy that you were going to pick to get in a fight with. I say that because I want to blow out of your mind forever the idea of a weak, namby-pamby Jesus. He was not. He was the most powerful male I have ever been in the presence of.[13]

The presence of Jesus, combined with the overwhelming sense of love and total acceptance that emanated from Him, filled Dr. Ritchie with an immense calm and an exhilarating sense of well-being. He was, however, astonished by the immediate transformation that had taken place. He went from the depths of despair into a place where he wasn't alone—but in the presence of a being who knew every minute detail of his life and totally loved and accepted him:

A moment before, I had been totally horrified. You don't know the devastating loneliness I was experiencing. The hopelessness. I had taken out my G.I. insurance shortly before this experience. I had thought that unless I was hit by a bullet I certainly was going to have three-score and ten. I barely had one score; I was dead three months prior to my twentieth birthday. I wasn't prepared to be dead at twenty years of age. But being in His presence—that saying that perfect love casts out fear says it all—this Being was the greatest incarnation of love you have ever seen. To be in His presence is to be devoid of any fear. To feel that somebody knows every minute detail about your life, and totally accepts and loves you, I never wanted to leave His side again under any circumstance to return to this realm. And I had some wonderful people and friends [to whom] to return.[14]

This heightened state of serenity and well-being that is felt so deeply in the near-death experience makes the prospect of returning to the physical world difficult indeed. George Ritchie said that, without question, he was never more alive than during the time of his near-death experience.

After his life review, Dr. Ritchie was taken to several different dimensions where souls reside after death. In one of the higher realms, he, too, understood what Edgar Cayce had said about everything that exists and manifests in the physical world having its origins in the spiritual dimensions:

I was taken to a place I call the "mental realm," for lack of a better word—it's a place where I heard the most beautiful music I have ever heard. Absolutely beautiful. I went into research labs—like an engineering school—where I couldn't begin to comprehend the instruments these beings were working on. It was like taking my seven-year-old grandson to the most sophisticated scientific labs at University of Virginia, and expecting him to comprehend. I simply could not understand. Well, ten years later [after the near-death experience], in 1952 or 1953, I saw a picture in *Life* magazine, of the first atomic powered plant. I felt the hair go right up the back of my neck because in this picture was a picture of an instrument I had seen these beings working on in 1943.

It was also in this realm where I went to a place like a seminary. The library of this particular university specialized in learning about God. The beings in this university had come from all over the universe. *All over the universe.* The library was larger than all the buildings put together in downtown Los Angeles. It housed the Holy Books of the Universe. All the Holy books that have ever been written in our world—including the Bible, Koran, Bhagavad Gita, Torah, etc.—would occupy only one little room of this vast library. Here I was standing beside the Christ, and had been taught that the Methodists, Presbyterians, and Baptists had the only way to Heaven. He was showing me beings I had never heard of, religions I had never heard of.[15]

This parallels the experience of Frances Banks, an Anglican nun, who visited a similar-sounding university and, after her death, described the beauty and wonder of it to her friend, author Helen Greaves. Frances was conveying the story of how, on the other side, one uses prayer and meditation to become at one with the Light of All—God—and the more one practices this (just as on our earth), the higher one rises in realms of consciousness. In this particular experience, Frances visited the sacred university—or a dimension like it—and detailed her experience:

I was transported (how I do not know) to another

Place, another Sphere, another "mansion" in this world . . . Suffice it to say that suddenly and immediately I was conscious of being in a great "atmosphere" of learning. I realised that I was in a university; yet it was much more than that, for there were Halls of Learning and a pervading atmosphere of Thought which thrilled my soul and satisfied a deep yearning in me. There were outer courts and beautiful vistas of gardens, where fountains of Light played. Here there were many souls, groups of students, sometimes surrounding One who appeared to be a Teacher, intent upon His discourse, or composed in deep meditation with Him . . . These here were of all types and from all nations . . . I was thrilled . . . Here, here I told myself, is my University of the Spirit, and the memory of my longing for the materialization of just such a university on earth filled me now with the new joy in this heavenly accomplishment . . . Now I *know* . . . that such Universities of Discourse and Study exist. *It is so* . . . The vision is still with me, complete and satisfying; the hope of further teaching and progress. I must make myself ready by continued service, as well as by facing myself and learning of my defects, ready for that transition to a sphere for which my whole soul yearns . . . [16]

The earth is but one small school in the universal scheme of creation. From Frances Banks's account and George Ritchie's experience, we have a correlation of experiences that indicates there are realms of higher learning; the education of the soul continues far beyond the realm of life in the material world. Dr. Ritchie was astonished at this "mental realm" he visited because it seemed to be composed of thousands of worlds, and millions of souls from all parts of the universe.

During a question-and-answer session at one of Ritchie's lectures, a young science professor commented on Dr. Ritchie's astonishment about the possibility of higher life forms.

"This scientist asked if I had any idea how many planets we [scientists] feel are equal, if not superior, to [earth] in development," Dr. Ritchie said. "I told him I had no idea—and he answered, 'Dr. Ritchie, there are thirteen million [suns]—just in our own Milky Way. If each sun in our own Milky Way has just one inhabited planet, there would be over thirteen million inhabited planets in our Milky Way.'"[17]

During his many stops on his lecture tours around the world, Dr. Ritchie re-creates his conversation with the younger professor, presenting the limitless possibilities for life outside of our earth plane. Dr. Ritchie also poses an interesting question to the audience:

> Do you think that a God who created a universe would be content with putting intelligent life on one little golfball-sized planet?[18]

Edgar Cayce said in a reading that the earth is but a small portion of God's creation:

> For the earth is only an atom in the universe of worlds! 5749-3

After visiting the mental realm, Jesus showed Dr. Ritchie a dimension that Dr. Ritchie likened to Heaven:

"What I was seeing literally blew my mind," he said. "We never went into this realm, were varying at about fifty to 150 feet above, but this was the first place we had been where the beings could see us as well as we saw them. And the beings in this place were growing like unto the Christ Himself in the amount of Light and Love they emitted. I called this place Heaven."[19]

Seeing this exquisite place, this light-filled world, where souls that looked just like human beings were becoming Christlike, was a crowning moment in Dr. Ritchie's near-death experience. And this particular facet of his message is most important to him.

"Having an experience like this," he said, " in the years that followed, I read everything I could of what Jesus said, or what He was reported to have said. If you read some of the things, He said, 'I am the first fruit of many that are to follow.' *He told you the truth.* The places I have seen are *us.* This is yours and mine, our ultimate destiny—not to be sent to a hell—but to become even as the Master Himself."[20]

The cycles of life and death, from earthly life to the unseen worlds, are preparation for a higher calling, a higher form of creation that the soul is becoming. It isn't possible for each soul to unfold and become like its Creator in one small lifespan on earth. It is a gradual unfoldment, an evolution through time and space, and many, many lives. Perhaps this is the message of the near-death experience—that we are much more than we know; we are much more sacred and spiritual than we think ourselves. Dr. Ritchie's near-death experience bears this truth out, and his message is both a warning and a reassurance: We will travel to the realm that we have built for ourselves after death. If that realm is one of earthly attachment and desire, we will find ourselves, immediately after death, chained to our attachments. But if we set our hearts to being of service, being about the business of learning to love, then we can be sure we will soar to the heights, unhindered by material concerns or attachment after physical death.

In the final stage of his near-death experience, Dr.

Ritchie was shown images and experiences that were prophetic in nature:

> Remember, [the time of this experience] was December 1943. But time as you and I know it does not exist. And the Christ opened up a corridor where I was able to see the coming of passing events. I saw increases in natural disasters—hurricanes, floods, tornadoes, earthquakes—all these were terrifically increasing. I saw explosions of a kind I have never seen before. What were these explosions? The bombs [that] were dropped over Hiroshima and Nagasaki. Seeing all of this in this corridor, I realized this planet could not withstand what I was seeing for very long. Another corridor was opened up and it started off the same way—hurricanes, tornadoes, floods, earthquakes—but a funny thing was happening. Instead of increasing in frequency and intensity they were getting less and less. Finally, I went into a time that I have never seen such peace and brotherly love. I think I was seeing the millennium. I was seeing the Christ back [on earth]. That corridor was then turned off. The Christ then turned to me and let me know, telepathically, that I would have to go back.[21]

Dr. Ritchie was shown two roads, two destinies of humankind—one that entailed violent upheavals (both natural and man-made), and one a world of peace and enlightenment. It was as if the Christ were saying to the world, via Dr. Ritchie, "It is up to you, people of the earth. Which road will you choose? The road of selfishness or the road of love?"

The memory of these events, told to an audience some fifty-five years later, is still very emotional for Dr.

Ritchie—particularly when he describes the moment that he knew he had to return to earth.

"I never, ever wanted to leave His side," he said. "And when I knew He meant to send me back, I made a fine leap to hang on to his neck! I never got there—he apparently stopped me in mid-air. The next thing I remember was seeing my fraternity ring on my hand, but I was seeing it through my physical eyes. The next time I was conscious, it was Christmas Eve. Indeed, the Christ had sent me back."[22]

Dr. Ritchie was sent back, along with thousands of others, seemingly for a divinely ordered work: to dispel the fears and misconceptions about life after death. Dr. Ritchie's experience, told to a twenty-one-year-old graduate student named Raymond Moody, indeed has shed tremendous light in a darkened world: Dr. Moody's book *Life After Life* has sold ten million copies and introduced the world to the first stages of life after physical death. It's as if God has taken selected individuals to see what lies beyond death's door and then sent them back to us, so that we will no longer fear death. George Ritchie believes that he was sent back to tell others that God is a god of love, not of vengeance or punishment:

We are loved beyond measure, beyond our wildest imaginings. The Being I encountered loved every unlovable thing about me. And I believe He wants others to both know this as a *fact* and to love our fellow human beings in equal measure. If we loved one another as He loves us, this material world would literally be a heaven on earth. We have the power to do this. It's all up to us.[23]

3

When Death Comes Early
or Unexpectedly

... pray oft for those who have passed on ... It is well ... Those
who have passed through God's other door are oft listening,
listening for the voice of those they have loved in the earth ...
Thy prayers direct [them] closer to that throne of love and
mercy, that pool of light, yea that river of God.

Edgar Cayce Reading 3954-1

ew things in life are more harrowing and painful
than when a loved one dies without warning or
when a parent must bury a child. The grief that accompanies such a loss may feel insurmountable. Such experiences seem to go against nature. In due season, it is
children who bury their parents, not the other way around.
Nor does it seem right that a loved one is taken away
without our having a chance to prepare for their going.

The loss of a child is particularly traumatic when the death comes without warning or illness. For many people, the death of a child is an event that propels them to begin a spiritual search for a deeper understanding of the enigmas of life and death. For many, unexpected or early death of a loved one marks the beginning of an illuminating unfoldment where, through seeking, they find a philosophy or spiritual understanding that opens the doorway to knowledge that the soul continues after death. In an epilogue to John Gunther's *Death Be Not Proud*, written after the death of his son Johnny, Frances Gunther, his wife, described the journey from the darkness of grief to a place where she discovered the light of spiritual healing:

> Yet at the end . . . when one has put away all the books, and all the words; when one is alone with oneself, when one is alone with God; what is left in one's heart? Just this: I wish we had loved Johnny more . . . Of course we loved Johnny very much . . . Loving Johnny more. What does it mean? What can it mean now? All parents who have lost a child will feel what I mean. Parents all over the earth who lost sons in the war have felt this kind of question and sought an answer. To me, it means loving life more, being more aware of life, of one's fellow human beings, of the earth. It means obliterating, in a curious but real way, the ideas of evil and hate and the enemy; and transmuting them, with the alchemy of suffering, into ideas of clarity and charity. It means caring more and more about other people, at home and abroad, all over the earth. It means caring more about God.[1]

Many sought guidance from Edgar Cayce when death

seemed to come too early or unexpectedly. Meeting Cayce, or receiving one of his psychic readings often marked the beginning of their understanding that life is continuous. To some parents, Cayce said that their child needed to be with them for only a short time; yet, in that short time, the soul experienced *an eternity* of love during its brief earthly life with the parents.

Cayce gave a reading for a terminally ill six-year-old girl. He advised the parents that they could be of great help to their dying daughter by reassuring her about the "beauty of the transition." Cayce also told the parents that the process of their daughter's passage through death was an *experience to provide growth and development to the soul*:

> So, only to keep the body as easy as possible and to maintain about this developing mind the *beauty* of transition, is the help as we find that may be given. A great deal might be given from the attitudes or phases of karmic forces, but for the material physical—to only make to the understanding mind the beauties of transition in the spiritual evolution of the mental and soul forces offers for the body and [the parents] that help, that stamina, that makes for a greater comprehending of the purposes of a soul's entrance into materiality, even to suffer under those experiences and to bring—as it appears—little opportunity of material help. Yet these experiences [the processes of dying] build into the warp and woof of each soul that which is a *continued* development for those that seek to know the ways of Divinity . . . Hence let each study to show *themselves* approved unto the Creative Forces. While these [circumstances] appear from the material view as very little, the hope and the promise that

have been given are sure . . . 1270-1

In the first part of the reading, Cayce was advising the parents to sit by the child's bedside and talk to the child in a soothing, reassuring manner. Whether the child was conscious or in a coma, the reassurances reached the *soul*, he said. What was most helpful was to tell the child to look for the Light, to tell her that she was loved, tell her that she was free from all pain and at complete peace. Cayce said such expressions of love aided the child in letting go more easily.

Without consideration of the soul's continued existence after death, the stages of dying can seem brutal and traumatic to the finite, conscious, logical mind. Both the gradual disintegration of the physical body during the final stages of a terminal illness and the unexpected death from trauma or sudden illness are extremely difficult and painful to both the dying person and to the family. In the above reading, Cayce told the parents that *true* understanding of the experience could not be gained unless the spirit was taken into consideration. In nature, there are patterns that can be compared to the stages of life, dying, and rebirth. The metamorphosis of a caterpillar to a butterfly symbolizes the journey through life into death. The caterpillar *dies* in order to become a new being. The caterpillar entombs itself in a cocoon, and then it goes through the stages of dying: The body darkens and withers, and then, at the moment of the caterpillar's death, the butterfly breaks out of the body it no longer needs and flies free, no longer confined to the tomb of its former body. In his novel, *Illusions—The Adventures of a Reluctant Messiah*, Richard Bach provided some words of wisdom to describe the spiritual side of the dying process: "What the caterpillar calls the end of the world, the master calls a butterfly."[2]

Just as the caterpillar must relinquish its shell and its cocoon, the dying process can be a time when the soul has the opportunity to gradually get rid of its "excess baggage" and let go of the earth-earthy patterns it will not need in the hereafter. Those who surround the dying can be of great help in aiding them in this transition. One way to help is by simply sitting by the bedside of a dying person, holding their hand, and telling them that they are in the companionship of their guardian angels and loved ones. In another reading, Cayce offered the following counsel to a family who was caring for a terminally ill loved one:

> There should be . . . those administrations of the mental and spiritual help which may be given by those who are near and close to the entity who may . . . make easier that journey which this entity soon must take. For life is not spent just because changes come about, but the greater opportunity for [the] soul-entity is to be released from the suffering. For in the same manner as He, who is the way, suffered, so must each individual meet that in the flesh; that we may know that the Savior bears with each soul that which will enable life, consciousness, to be a continued experience. Thus, it behooves those who seek help, even, to be patient, to be gentle, to be kind to others. For this entity needs not, [except] the assurance . . . 5194-1

When a loved one faces death at a young age or unexpectedly, the normal reaction of survivors is to want to keep that person alive as long as possible because we need them here. But the most important work we have to do when a loved one is facing imminent death is to help them mentally and spiritually in making the transition. It's not uncommon for distressed family members to keep a dying person alive through artificial means, rather than letting them die with peace and dignity. With the rapid advancements in medical technology, it is now even possible to keep the body alive by machines when there is no brain wave activity. Most of us probably will face the situation at some point in our lives where we will have the opportunity to, as Cayce put it, help "the soul entity . . . to be released from the suffering . . . " Or we can choose to have our loved ones hooked to machines to maintain physical life without regard for the *quality* of that life. Oftentimes, well-meaning family members gather around the bedside of a dying person and keep them from letting go; they hold the person back through their thoughts and desires. The deathbed vigil can be an opportunity for the family to mentally and spiritually be a force to help the soul *let go*. Particularly when the soul is in a comatose state, the thoughts, the feelings, and desires of family and friends have a direct impact upon the mind and soul of the dying. In *The Tibetan Book of Living and Dying*, author Sogyal Rinpoche offers specific guidelines for helping to make the transition easier for the dying person:

> If you are attached and cling to the dying person, you can bring him or her a lot of unnecessary heartache and make it very hard for the person to let go and die peacefully. Sometimes the dying person can linger on many months or weeks longer than doctors expected and experience tremendous physical suffering . . . for such a person to be able to let go and die peacefully, he or she needs to hear two explicit verbal assurances from loved ones. First, they must give the person permission to die, and second they must reassure the person that [the survivors]

will be all right after he or she has gone, and that
there is no need to worry about them. When people
ask me how to best give someone permission to die,
I tell them to imagine themselves standing by the
bedside of the person they love and saying with the
deepest and most sincere tenderness: "I am here
with you and I love you. You are dying, and that is
completely natural; it happens to everyone. I wish
you could stay here with me, but I don't want you to
suffer any more. The time we have had together has
been enough and I shall always cherish it. Please
now don't hold onto life any longer. Let go. I give
you my full and heartfelt permission to die. You are
not alone, now or ever. You have all my love . . . "[3]

Again, these words can be spoken to a dying person
regardless of whether the patient is conscious or in a
coma. Whether the person is conscious or unconscious,
the soul is still very sensitive to the thoughts and feelings of people who surround the body. Because of this, it
is of vital importance that everyone who visits a dying
person be careful of both thoughts and words. Those
surrounding the dying individual have a great responsibility: Their thoughts, beliefs and desires, as Rinpoche
indicated, can make the death difficult and traumatic or
enable the process to be peaceful, beautiful, and easy.

After the death of a loved one, especially when the
death comes unexpectedly or prematurely, where are we
to turn for relief and healing? Cayce recommended that
through turning attention within and seeking guidance
through introspection or meditation, every soul may
come to understand the continuity of life and may *experience* the closeness of those loved ones who have passed
on. The following question and answer is relevant to this
practice and was given for a woman struggling with the

process of grief, following the death of her husband:

> (Q) Is there any message you could give regarding her husband, who has passed beyond, that would help her?
> (A) These . . . may be best had through that introspection of self in those periods when one may turn to the within and seek that counsel, that at-oneness with those who are in the borderland; for *all* is well in that oneness of the purposes as may be accomplished . . . through the mental changing, or guiding, that the *spirit* may work aright. 5488-1

In other words, help and assistance are available from *within* the self, not outside. And turning attention within—the acts of focusing on spiritual communion and asking for such—bring the soul into attunement with the Divine and awaken a sense of oneness and harmony. By doing so, according to this reading, Cayce said it brings us into closer communion with our deceased loved ones who are in the beyond, or what Cayce called "the borderland"—a dimension of consciousness where there is interaction between those who are in the material world and those who have passed on.

In 1934, a young college student died unexpectedly. She was attending Barnard College in New York City, and her body was found several floors beneath her dormitory window. It was evident that her death resulted from a fall from the window, but officials didn't know if the girl was pushed to her death, committed suicide, or accidentally fell. These unanswered questions deepened the family's shock and grief and prompted the girl's aunt to seek out Edgar Cayce. She was acquainted with Cayce's health and spiritual readings. It was her hope that he could answer the questions surrounding the girl's death.

The case was a peculiar one for Cayce. Unlike readings he had given for other people, reading 4938-1 would be his first attempt to obtain a *post-mortem* reading. He readily agreed to try to help, but cautioned that this type of reading was uncharted territory and the results might not be satisfactory. He was, after all, attempting to "locate"—psychically—an individual who had passed beyond the physical dimensions of time and space.

On October 28, 1935, Edgar Cayce, his wife Gertrude, secretary Gladys Davis, and the dead girl's aunt gathered in Cayce's den for the reading. After a brief session of prayer and meditation, which was held before each reading period, Cayce lay down on the couch and began to enter the sleeplike state that everyone hoped would enable his mind and soul to connect with the circumstances of the girl's death. Cayce placed his hands over his closed eyes and waited for the "signal"—a brilliant flash of white light he glimpsed at the point of entering the trance state. He lowered his hands and folded them over his solar plexus. As Cayce's eyelids began to flutter, Gertrude recited the suggestion requesting psychic information:

"You will have before you the entity known as [Ellen Brown][4]," Mrs. Cayce said, "who was in one of the dormitories at Barnard College, New York City, in the early morning hours of Saturday, September 28th. You will tell us what you are privileged to tell, and that which will be helpful to those closely concerned. You will then answer the questions that may be asked by her aunt, present in this room."

Edgar Cayce lay completely still on the couch, breathing deeply. After a few moments, he made a statement that startled everyone in the room.

"Yes, we are with the entity here," Cayce said, indicating contact was made with the dead girl. " . . . This, as may be and should be understood by those who are interested was an accident—and not premeditated or purposed by the entity."

In other words, Ellen's unexpected death wasn't an act of self-destruction nor was she murdered. He continued:

The environs or surroundings that made for these happenings, in a material world, are with the entity in the present, making for better understandings.

Those that are near and dear to [Ellen], *to make for more understandings—condemn no one, nor the circumstance* [emphasis added]. Neither mourn for those who are at rest.

There is gradually coming the awakening. This, to be sure, is an experience through which the entity, [Ellen], is passing in the present . . . [The experience] is making for a helpfulness in [Ellen's] understanding and comprehending of that which is the experience . . .

Let thy prayer be: *In thy mercy, in thy goodness, Father, keep her. Make for those understandings in my experience, in her experience, that we may draw nearer and nearer together in that oneness of purpose that His love is known more and more in the minds and hearts of those that are in the positions of opportunities for being a channel, a messenger, in the name of Christ. Amen.*

At this point in the reading, Cayce asked for questions: "Is she happy, and does she understand where she is?" the aunt asked.

"As given," Cayce responded, "there is the awakening, and there is the understanding coming more and more. And soon to the aunt may come the awareness of her presence near . . . Let the prayer as given be held occasionally, especially in the early mornings."

In reviewing this reading, what has been startling to many students of Cayce's psychic readings is the use of the word "accident" relative to the girl's death. It is important to realize that Cayce gave psychic readings *in the language the individual seeking help could comprehend.* Cayce's use of the word "accident" did not mean it wasn't time for her transition from the earth; it was a term he used to remove all doubt in the family's mind that Ellen had not committed suicide.

Although Cayce didn't give information about *why* the girl passed on so early in her life, he assured the aunt that the soul they knew as Ellen was still very much alive and still very much in need of help from the family, in the form of prayer. Cayce never minimized the power of prayer, particularly for those who have died:

> Prayer for those who are seeking a way, *the* way to the Light, aids ever. As ye meditate—as ye pray— for as thy body is indeed the temple of the living God, there He hath promised to meet thee . . . pray that there may be the light, the help needed, that they [the deceased] may be guided in the way and manner which will bring all together in the way as He, thy Lord, would have it. 2280-1

Prayer and meditation bring us closer to a state of at-onement with the Divine and with loved ones who have passed on, and it helps heal the loneliness of the grieving process. Cayce told the aunt during the reading, " . . . soon to the aunt may come the awareness of her presence near." You, too, might have the experience of sensing the presence of your loved ones by turning your attention within, for this can come as we focus upon the continuity of life and meditate upon the principle that there is no separation between the here and the hereafter. Engaging in conversation with loved ones who have passed on is also a great help to the living and to the person on the other side. For the grieving to heal more quickly, it's important to affirm and reaffirm that the soul is eternal and cannot die. After focusing on this in deep meditation or contemplation, ask for divine help, strength, and guidance so that you can experience this understanding to help yourself and the person who has died. The best time to enter into the silence is in the early morning hours, just as Cayce suggested for the girl's aunt to pray at this period. The optimal hours for meditation and prayer, according to Cayce, are between 2:00 and 3:00 a.m. Many people have reported visionary encounters, light experiences, and communion with deceased loved ones when they pray and meditate in the early morning hours.

> . . . pray oft for those who have passed on . . . Those who have passed through God's other door are oft listening, listening for the voice of those they have loved in the earth. The nearest and dearest thing they have been conscious of in earthly consciousness . . . thy prayers direct such an one closer to that throne of love and mercy, that pool of light, yea that river of God. 3954-1

The bonds of love do not end at physical death. Our thoughts and emotions affect the transitioning soul after death just as our words and behavior affected them in life. We can assist and reassure them by focusing upon prayers and thoughts of love and light and a deep desire that they reach the Light unimpeded.

Cayce gave another reading for a bereaved family who

had a member die rather unexpectedly. Anne Spencer[5] came to Edgar Cayce seeking information about her mother, who had died unexpectedly from a heart attack. Because the mother hadn't been ill prior to her death, the experience was even more traumatic for Anne and her family. When death comes without warning, family members often feel much has been left undone and unsaid, and there is regret and grief over this unfinished business.

The reading given for Anne and her family is one that is most unusual as well as inspiring. Cayce described the spiritual reasons for the mother's passing *and* he communicated a message from the mother to the family. Cayce occasionally acted as a medium while giving his psychic readings. Such experiences occurred when the attunement of Edgar Cayce, those present in the room, and the person about whom he was giving the reading was in perfect accord. Cayce's ability to do this was very similar to tuning in to a radio station frequency. When the frequency was just right, the deceased was able to give messages through Cayce. For Anne and her family, the message that came through Cayce was very powerful and very healing.

It was a warm day in July 1937, when Anne followed Gladys, Gertrude, and Edgar Cayce into the reading room. Cayce stretched out on the couch and closed his eyes. Gertrude read the suggestion to him as he entered the trance state:

> You will have before you the circumstances and conditions surrounding the death of [Margaret Spencer][6] . . . June 8, 1937; together with the various members of her family and the questions resulting from her sudden death; especially the questions of [. . .] her daughter, who requests a Reading on these

conditions. You will give that which may be helpful to the family at this time and answer the questions which they have presented.

EC: Yes, we have those circumstances and conditions attending the separation of the body and soul of Margaret Spencer. In giving that as would be helpful and constructive in the experience of each member of this family:

As has been so aptly said, her life, her work, her love is an example of Christian faith and fortitude ... The body was so tired from the cares of the material world that the physical reactions were in the heart; that had been so ready to open itself to the needs of each, not only of the family but to all that knew, that even were acquainted with the body. Yet, [she] grew so weary with these cares that He, in His love, saw fit to let the separation come; that the soul might in peace *rest* in the arms of Him who is her Savior—JESUS!

Hence you each should take the lesson of that courage, of that patience, of that forbearance, of that longsuffering, as part of *your* own lives; and let it become—as she manifested—the *experience* of everyday life, in the dealings and in the associations with the fellow man. The physical condition that wrought the change [physical death] was the engorgement of the arteries between the heart and the liver. The dregs of hardships, of trials, became heavy. As to the message that she would leave, that she would give to each [family member]: ...

To [. . .] [1st daughter]: Keep the care that has been given thee, even as a good shepherdess watching over the flock, even as He has shown in His ways.

To [. . .] [2nd daughter]: Care for the home. Let that be thy part, thy mission, now. When there are

the changes that are natural to come, these then will
be a share of another; but keep thou the home for
Papa, for [son], for [the youngest daughter].

To [. . .] [3rd daughter]: Let those things wherein
oft reproved, oft directed, be kept in that loving faith
that has been thy outlook upon life. For hold fast to
the things that bespeak of the true spiritual life; for
in these ye find peace and happiness and joy.

To [. . .] [son]: Attend thy father's needs. Be his
right hand. If it is in keeping with thy inner self, prepare thy ways in the preparations in school for the
activities of life itself. But look after him.

To the *baby* [. . .]: Let [the three older sisters],
keep watchful care with thee. Know, as in the experience of those that have lived and know the pitfalls;
know those things that make one weary; but hold
fast to that which is good.

And may the blessings of the Father, through the
love as shown in the Christ, guide each of you.
Through the vicissitudes of life, through all the
shadows, through all the disappointments, through
all the sorrows, know He is near—and will hold thee
by the hand. We are through. 1408-2

We see through the readings an emerging larger view
of the nature of death and dying. Margaret's death was
traumatic for the family, and yet the reading said her
death was *a blessing.* As Cayce said, " . . . [she] grew so
weary . . . that He, in his love, saw fit to let the separation
come; that the soul might in peace *rest . . .* "

"Know that life is a continuous experience," Cayce
said in another reading, "and as there is a consciousness
in sleep that is not physical—in the sense of physical
awareness—so there is a consciousness in the same
manner when the physical is entirely laid aside . . . Then,

there should not be sorrow and sadness in those periods when the physical turmoils and strifes of the body are laid aside, for the moment, for the closer walk with Him ... and then when the shadows ... begin to close about, and there is a meeting at the river, there will be indeed no sorrow when this barque puts out to sea." (1824-1)

4

An Account of the Soul's
Journey After Death

*. . . it is not all of life to live, nor all of death to die; for one is the
beginning of the other . . .*   Edgar Cayce Reading 2842-2

Author Helen Greaves had many psychic experiences
during her lifetime. She understood that the sixth
sense naturally develops through regular meditation
and prayer. Little did she realize that her development
would enable her to be a "bridge between the worlds"
and chronicle the after-death experiences of her longtime friend and spiritual mentor, Frances Banks. Frances
was an Anglican nun, missionary, author, and teacher.
She and Helen quickly developed a spiritual bond when
they met through the Churches' Fellowship for Psychical and Spiritual Studies. Both women were writers,
speakers, and researchers in the psychic sciences. For

the last eight years of Frances's life, she and Helen conducted spiritual and psychic studies in England. They formed a spiritual study group and explored the inner worlds of the soul and spirit through disciplined prayer and meditation. After a time, the two women began to have psychic visions and experiences, including periods in which they seemed to communicate with the dead. Their undertaking was not for mere curiosity; they believed that deep meditation and prayer were the inner journey that brought the soul closer to the Creator. Helen and Frances held sacred their many psychic experiences; they understood that these experiences were "signs along the way" that they were growing closer in awareness to the Creator.

Frances and Helen believed that humanity stood on the threshold of a great reawakening and rebirth; they envisioned a world where people understood that clairvoyance, telepathy, and communication between the living and the dead were normal facets of the spiritual life. It was their hope that their spiritual studies would eventually help others who were in need—those who were afraid of dying, those who had lost their faith, those who felt apart from God. This high spiritual intention seemed to be the power that bridged the distance between the living and the dead and enabled Frances, after her death, to return to Helen and speak of her journey.

Frances began telepathically communicating with Helen just days after her death, instructing Helen to "take dictation." The purpose of Frances's communication was to publish her own account so the world might know that life continued after physical death. Her detailed after-life journey was published in 1969 by Helen Greaves, entitled *Testimony of Light*. In her introduction to the book, Helen said that her communications from

Frances were a natural continuance of the spiritual work
the two women had shared prior to Frances's death:

> Frances . . . has shown to be possible that which
> she always advocated so strongly, *that psychic and
> spiritual communication are but different levels of
> one spiral* . . . She was convinced [during her earthly
> life] of the fact of communication with the spiritual
> worlds and of the reality of the higher self in each
> one of us. She trusted implicitly in the survival of
> mind and personality beyond death . . . In the testi-
> mony which follows, Frances continues her mis-
> sion. She has shown her experience of death and
> the change into a new conception of living, illus-
> trating this with poignant stories of the effects of the
> death-change on others with whom she has been
> brought into contact. She gives us freely of her fur-
> ther knowledge of the progress of the soul out-
> wards, upwards and forwards into Divinity.[1]

Frances was diagnosed with terminal cancer at age
seventy-two. Her years of spiritual study prepared her to
go through the stages of her terminal illness with serenity and peace. Their spiritual work also helped Helen to
have the strength to let go of her friend and colleague
and to get through the last months of Frances's life. Due
to their psychic sensitivity, both women became aware
that there were unseen presences and spiritual helpers
surrounding them in the hospital. One of the invisible
beings was Frances's deceased friend and mentor, Mother
Florence, who had been Frances's Mother Superior years
earlier during her teaching and missionary work in
South Africa.

"When Frances lay in a London hospital," Helen
wrote, "I told her that I felt Mother Florence was with her.

I recall her calm smile. 'I know!' Frances said. 'Last night I saw Mother Florence distinctly by my bed.'"[2]

Frances had approached her eventual death, even before she was diagnosed with cancer, as a natural progression of the life cycle. Because she believed that life continued after physical death, she viewed the dying process as a spiritual "birth."

"Frances Banks died, as she had lived," Helen said, "fully conscious of what she was doing . . . She astonished the good Scottish doctor who attended her at the last by saying cheerfully, a day or so before she lapsed into a coma: 'Good-bye, Doctor. See you in the next world!'"[3]

Helen stayed close as her friend was dying, meditating and praying that Frances's transition to the Light would be one of great peace and beauty. Frances was semicomatose during the final days, but was free from pain.

"Frances was propped up by pillows, ill and shrunken," Helen wrote. "She was very still except for the labored indrawing of her breath. I stood for a moment at the end of the bed, watching her. Slowly her eyes opened. Recognition dawned. She smiled without speaking . . . After a minute, without opening her eyes, she murmured in a dreamy voice, 'It's all right, my dear. *The Change has started.*'"[4]

Frances then lapsed into unconsciousness and died the following day, November 2, 1965. Three days later, she contacted Helen:

I felt Frances's *mind* impinging on mine. Words dropped into my thoughts which did not come from my consciousness. I knew that her discarnate mind and my incarnate one had linked together again in telepathic communication . . . Frances

would now be able to demonstrate the next life, of
which she had written and spoken; to expound with
authority on the subject which had been close to
her heart; the reality of Life Everlasting; the continued progress of the spirit . . .

I sat down, took my pen and began to write . . .
words, thoughts, sentences tumbled out on to the
paper. It was almost as though I took dictation. Yet
this was *not* automatic writing. I was perfectly in
control. I could *feel* [Frances's] mind using mine.[5]

For the next eighteen months, Helen sat quietly and
listened to Frances's voice, transcribing verbatim the account of the many worlds that exist beyond the veil of
three-dimensional life.

Many questions regarding the accuracy and appropri-
ateness of communicating with the dead were addressed
in the Cayce readings. Cayce indicated that such communications can only occur when there is mutual coop-
eration between the worlds:

(Q) Is it possible for those who have passed into
the spirit plane to at all times communicate with
those in the earth plane?

(A) Yes and no. The *necessary* way or mode must
be prepared . . . Those in the astral plane are not
always ready. Those in the physical plane are not
always ready . . . What conditions arise . . . that we in
the physical plane are not ready? The *mind!* What
conditions arise that we in the astral plane are not
ready? . . . the willingness of that *individual* to communicate . . . The willingness and the desire from
both is necessary for the perfect communication,
see? Illustrate this same condition by . . . that called
radio, or of that called [telephone] . . . Necessary for

the perfect union that each be in accord. In other words, we find many in the astral plane *seeking* to give force active in the material [world]. Many in the material [world] *seeking* to delve into the astral. They must be made one, would they bring the better [information]. 5756-4

The attunement that Helen and Frances had developed together over the course of eight years had created a channel through which Frances could speak about her life after death to her friend Helen. In many ways Helen was like a radio receiving station, and Frances communicated with her through the etheric wavelength. In their first session, Frances described what happened to her immediately after she left her body:

As soon as I was able to bring myself to a conscious state of mind, after my withdrawal from my worn-out body, I knew that I was the *same in essence*... yet not the same. With a flash of realization I decided that I must be stone deaf, for I could no longer hear any of the usual sounds of everyday life, the chatter and movement of human beings around me ... There were no noises in this new consciousness. One of my first recollections was "I am still conscious. *The Change has taken place*... but I cannot hear, neither can I see!" ... I seemed to have lost my identity... It was a strange, almost eerie experience, for the name I had borne for over seventy years eluded me ... At length I recall telling myself to "give it up and go to sleep" and, in a way, this is what I must have done ... I remembered nothing more. How long this went on I have no possible way of knowing... perhaps in earth time, for a very short space ... Next when I came back to consciousness I

seemed to be pulling myself up out of a thin sea of
silver . . . those are the only words I can use to describe the experience . . . And the first face I saw was
. . . my dear Mother in religion—Mother Florence
. . . I was so overwhelmed I couldn't speak . . . I am
now lying in a bed, high up on a terrace, that looks
out over a vast sunlit plain. It is a beautiful scene,
and so restful . . . I am recuperating from the illness
which brought disintegration to my physical body
. . . Souls are brought here from earth and from
other places (but I do not know much of those
places)—when they are ready . . . After the Change
was over and I was free of my earthly "covering" I
"woke up" here in this hospital of the Rest Home . . .
I opened my eyes . . . or I came back to consciousness . . . and there was Mother Florence just as . . . I
had remembered for so many years. She took my
hand [and] said, "So you have arrived safely?" . . . [6]

Frances's description of her transition after death is
very similar to the stages of birth and growth in the
physical world. Frances passed through a period of unconsciousness and loss of identity, and then gradually
became aware of herself as an individual being, aware of
her surroundings in the fourth dimension. These stages
are not unlike being born into the physical world: We are
each physically born into this world as an infant, without full conscious awareness of our whereabouts. As
time goes by, the baby begins to learn to communicate,
to walk, and to think. As this stage passes, the body and
mind gradually become aware, and the self-aware personality emerges. The soul constantly grows through a
myriad of life experiences in the material world, ever
changing and growing through the process. Edgar Cayce
said that the gradual growth and unfoldment in the ma-

terial world are but a shadow or reflection of the stages of growth and development that occur after physical death:

> Passing from the material consciousness [at death] to a spiritual . . . consciousness oft does an entity or being not become conscious of that about it; much in the same manner as an entity born into the [earth] only becomes conscious gradually of . . . time and space for the material or third dimensional plane. In the passage the entity becomes conscious, or the recognition of being in a fourth or higher dimensional plane takes place, much in the same way as the consciousness is gained in the material [world]. For . . . that we see manifested in the material plane is but a shadow of that in the spiritual plane . . .
>   . . . that as called death . . . is only a transition . . . through God's other door . . . Hence the [soul] development is through the planes of experience that an entity may become one *with* the first cause . . .
>   For, in the comprehension of no time, no space, no beginning, no end, there may be the glimpse of what simple transition or birth into the material is; as passing through the outer door into another consciousness. Death in the material plane is passing through the outer door into a consciousness . . . that partakes of what the entity, or soul, has done with its spiritual truth in its manifestation in the other sphere. 5749-3

Frances awoke after physical death and found herself in the presence of her mentor, Mother Florence. Because a great portion of her life was spent in spiritual activities and service under the mentorship of Mother Florence,

her soul naturally gravitated to the place in consciousness where her mentor resided. Frances become ori-
ented to her after-death environment very rapidly due
to her years of preparation and study. The knowledge
and understanding she gained in her physical life about
the spiritual worlds literally went with her after death,
speeding her orientation. We can see this principle at
work in the physical world in the lives of children: Some
children become adept at walking and talking faster than
others; some are able to do mathematics and spelling
more rapidly than others. It is the same for every soul
after physical death.

The more we develop a spiritual consciousness during physical life—through study, meditation, prayer,
etc.—the more easily we will be able to pass through the
transition at physical death. By the same token, when
physical life is expended solely in pursuit of earthly grati-
fication and fulfilling material desires, it takes a longer
period for the soul to awaken after physical death. What
we build in the earthly life through our heart's desires
and thoughts creates the fabric of where we will find ourselves after physical death.

"By man's thoughts and inspirations he weaves for
himself his future place in this dimension," Frances said.
"This is logical Law. In the earth life he can build a fa-
cade about himself. Here he has no such mask. He is
known here for what he is, and for what *his inner subjec-
tive* life has made him. 'Lay up for yourselves treasures
in heaven' may be taken as having a *factual* meaning."[7]

It is safe to say that we *become* the essence of the
thoughts, desires, and activities we created during our
lives on earth. Consequently, every soul must, after the
death transition, go through a period of letting go of
material attachments, desires, habits, etc. The fewer
material attachments and desires we cultivate during

the physical existence, the more easily the soul is able to move into its new spiritual environment after death.

"We move into that state of consciousness [after death] by the way we think and by what we are trying to satisfy," Hugh Lynn Cayce once said. "We are so closely tied to the earth that we don't even realize for a little while that we are dead, but in no time, then, we begin to awaken . . . We maintain a mental set, a mental pattern [during physical life], and we carry it over with us. We have the same ideas, the same attitudes."[8]

"For do not consider for a moment . . . " Edgar Cayce said in a reading, "that an individual soul-entity passing from an earth plane as a Catholic, a Methodist, an Episcopalian, is something else because he is dead! He's only a dead Episcopalian, Catholic or Methodist!" (254-92)

Frances Banks was still an Anglican nun after her death; her attitudes were the same and so were her beliefs. She described to Helen Greaves the experience that she was undergoing to remove the material boundaries she had created during her life on earth:

> I am trying to shed some of the clutter of the personality. We all have to do that . . . And there are three ways in which to carry it out here. By self-judgment and true assessment of experience; by service to one's fellows; and by aspiration. Not so different, you will say, from the earth life after all! I can express it best in this thought; the "subjective" or inner content of my thoughts, aspirations and desires here and now will fashion the "objective" place to which I will pass on the next stage of my journey; just as the inner life of the soul within the body-mind on earth decides the first future "home" on this level. More and more important therefore and invaluable, is the inner life of meditation and

contemplation and at-one-ment with Divine Beauty in Truth.[9]

One of the most important facets of Frances's account of life on the other side was the assurance that *no soul goes through the death transition alone.* She said there are helper spirits who are present when the soul separates from the body. When a soul is readying to make its final journey, to leave the body behind, relatives on the other side are alerted that a family member is on the way. As the soul awakens after the death transition, it often finds itself surrounded by people whom the soul knew and loved while on earth:

> Our work is to be on hand when those newly arrived entities awake to awareness. [On occasion], ours are the first "countenances" they see; ours are the words of comfort, assurance and welcome . . . Many [souls] will not accept the fact of death, or prefer to consider that they still dream . . . The weary souls, the frightened souls, the ignorant and the "fallen" souls, together with those who have been "rescued" from the "Land of Shadows" require understanding and explanation . . . and there are some to whom Survival [of death] has to be explained, even demonstrated. Many will not accept the fact of death . . . [10]

The souls who have the easiest transition, according to Frances, are children. Because they have only been on the earth for a short time, their souls are still very acclimated to the spiritual worlds they recently departed to incarnate into the earth. Infants and children who die young wake up very quickly after the death transition, according to Frances, and they are always in the companionship of benevolent spirits. She emphasized this many times in the transcripts, because of the immense grief parents undergo in the death of a child. Frances told a beautiful story of a young girl named Jeannie, who had died very young from complications of polio. Prior to her death, Jeannie had always dreamed of becoming a dancer and had trained from a very young age—and showed a marked degree of talent. Unfortunately, polio crippled Jeannie's left leg—it withered, shortened, and she was permanently crippled. She underwent many painful operations without success. Her weakened physical condition, combined with the mental anguish of knowing she would never dance again, left her spiritually and physically depleted. Just after her twelfth birthday, Jeannie died from pneumonia. Frances was waiting on the other side with Mother Florence when the little girl came to waking consciousness after dying. Jeannie was momentarily distressed; she didn't realize she had died and thought she was in the hospital for yet another torturous operation. The following account is Frances's description of what transpired when Jeannie came to waking consciousness after death:

"Please, please don't make me have any more operations," Jeannie said to Mother Florence.

"You are only in our Home for a rest . . . You're going to be quite well again, Jeannie . . . quite well."

"No," she said, "I'll never be well. I've got a shrunken leg."

"Not now, Jeannie," Frances said, "Not any more. Your leg is well, quite well and strong . . . We're going to teach you to run and play and dance here, Jeannie."

Jeannie stared . . . She ran her hands up and down her calves, over the ankles, fingering the bones of the feet carefully and then back to the knees . . .

"Is it a miracle?" she asked in an awed voice.

"You could call it a miracle," Mother Florence answered . . . "supposing you get up and stand . . . "

"Will it hurt?" Jeannie asked.

"No. You won't have any pain. You'll never have that old pain again, Jeannie."

Frances and Mother Florence gently lifted Jeannie and raised her to her feet. At first Jeannie was terrified; she had full remembrance of how difficult it had been for her to stand without support or braces. Slowly, the little girl stood erect, balancing on both feet.

"It's true. It's true. It *is* a miracle," Jeannie said, crying tears of happiness. "I shall walk again. I'm well. I'm like other girls!"[11]

Frances acted as Jeannie's guardian angel during the time she spent recuperating. Like many souls, Jeannie didn't realize that she was dead for some time. She imagined that she was immersed in some wonderful dream, a dream far removed from the pain of the physical world. In a place we might call Paradise, Frances accompanied Jeannie to hillsides filled with flowers, where the child ran, jumped, and danced. After a time, Jeannie came to the realization that the Paradise where she found herself was no dream:

"I've realized that I'm not dreaming," Jeannie said to Frances. "We're all dead. That's true, isn't it?"

"Yes. It's true, Jeannie," Frances answered, "but you see we're really more alive than ever. You've only got rid of your sick old body and found a new one . . . "

"I suppose this is Life Everlasting?" Jeannie asked.

"We have always been in Life Everlasting, Jeannie,

even when we were on earth," Frances said. "Our souls, our true Selves, always have lived from experience to experience. This is only another *part* of the experience ... "

"Mother Florence says when I'm ready I'll go to the Halls of Beauty, that's in another part of Heaven. She says I'll see the greatest dancers in all the world there. She says I'll learn to dance ... and that I'll be able to join with these others in the great Dance Festivals. Do you believe that Sister?"

"Mother Florence knows much more about the Spheres than I do," Frances said.

"Oh, it will be lovely! Of course, I'll miss you and ... Mother Florence and everybody, but I want to go so much. I must go soon ... "[12]

Jeannie had adapted quickly to the life after death. She embraced every facet of her life in the hereafter with great joy and enthusiasm. Her heart's desire to dance was, Frances realized, truly a divine gift. Watching Jeannie, she glimpsed a facet of the Divine she had overlooked during her earthly life. True, Frances was an exemplary teacher, a spiritual pioneer, and had gained much in soul development while on earth—but there was more to life than working, searching, and study:

She adjusted to this new life with all the flexibility of a child's unspoiled nature. To her everything was a revelation ... That child, by the fine quality of her nature, had taught me much. Beauty as such, in the creative arts of dancing and movement, had been absent from my earth life altogether. Now I realized how much I had missed. For Beauty is surely an attribute of God . . . and the art of the dance is a manifestation of that attribute. I hope that I shall see Jeannie in her Hall of Beauty Festivals sometime. It will be a great and moving moment . . . [13]

Frances found her position to help newly arrived souls very fulfilling indeed. As a result of her one-on-one experience with many souls, Frances attained a higher state of consciousness and awareness.

Edgar Cayce once said that heaven is not a place that we go to, it is a place that we *grow* to, on the arm of someone we have helped. Frances's testimony illustrated this principle in many accounts in *Testimony of Light*, and one of the most striking was her experience with a woman and child who arrived on the other side at the same time. The woman, a missionary, and her foster child were both killed when there was an uprising in the country where they lived:

> They had arrived here together, for it seemed that even in the period of [death] transition to this plane she had held the child to her with love . . . Her first words, when she became conscious of her surroundings, were "I knew I would wake up amongst Sisters. Thank God! It is wonderful!" There was no question of surviving the terrible ordeal through which she had met death; there were no recriminations, no fears and most impressive of all, no hatreds. She exuded unselfish love.[14]

When the woman realized the small child, Laki, was with her, safely "sleeping" (as Frances put it), she was overcome with joy. She told Frances and the other beings that she had promised Laki's parents she would look after the child as her own. Laki's natural parents had died several years before. Now that the woman and Laki were on the other side, she asked the Guides to help Laki be reunited with his birth family from the previous life. When the woman's heartfelt request was made to the overseers of the realm, Frances and the Guides set out to find the parents. This was accomplished by focused concentration of the spirit guides—they entered a state of deep communion, and petitioned the souls called the "Great Ones," and sent the request to the higher realms:

> They "concentrated" asking for help from the Great Ones . . . sent out their thoughts to contact the "beam" on whose ray these souls were abiding. And a contact was made. A messenger arrived with a guide, and little Laki went on to his rightful place. His foster mother was overjoyed for she knew that she would be able to visit him and help him as she had done when in the physical body . . . Laki rejoined his people; our missionary rested with us. To me she was a lesson without words! How much I learned from her! For she was indeed one of the Chosen.[15]

Frances described the beautiful scenario of the missionary woman who, after knowing that Laki was safe with his family, was ready to leave the way station where Frances resided and depart for the higher realms:

> Mother Florence . . . and our missionary were talking together on the terrace here when Mother Florence observed that her patient appeared to have gone into a deep contemplation. They remained still and silent. Mother felt a great Presence as of an Angel of Light with them; she held her soul in quiet expectation. Then the Light grew stronger about them, the air more potent, and there was a

"feeling of music." Her missionary friend, she said, impulsively stirred, put out her hand and touched Mother Florence. "Thank you and bless you for all your kind reception of me . . . How splendid your work is here! And I realize that it is entirely voluntary. But your true place is waiting for you all when you have completed your service. May I often come and visit with you?" Mother Florence felt that she had no words with which to reply except "God bless you." The Light grew and multiplied about them and Mother said that her eyes were only able to perceive the Light and nothing more. She felt herself swept upwards into enlightenment. When her "spirit returned" (those are *her* words), our missionary had left. She had gone to her rightful Place. Love had been translated to Higher Spheres . . . [16]

From Frances's testimony through Helen Greaves, we can begin to glean an understanding that the passage through death is merely *a first stage*, a birth to a higher form of life and consciousness. The soul does not begin at birth or end at death. Cayce likened the soul passing through the stages of life and physical death to the passing of seasons, from spring to summer, summer to fall, fall to winter. As we live and pass through the seasons of our material world, we don't experience a beginning or end—only a transition from one to the other. Such is the nature of our passing from the material world to the spiritual dimensions. In the passage, we grow in experience, grace, knowledge, and—most importantly—we grow higher in consciousness to eventually become aware that our soul is eternally part of the Creator. According to Cayce, that is the eventual destiny of every soul—to be an individual, and also an integral part of the Divine. Edgar Cayce said:

For life, in its continuity, is that experience of the soul or entity—including its soul, its spirit, its superconscious, its subconscious, its physical consciousness . . . in that as its *development* goes through the various experiences takes on more and more of that ability of knowing itself to be itself, yet a portion of the great whole, or the one Creative Energy that is in and through all. 900-426

5

Reassurances
from Beyond

The truly wise mourn neither for the living nor for the dead.
There was never a time when I did not exist, nor you, nor any
of these kings. Nor is there any future in which we shall cease
to be . . . Bodies are said to die but That which possesses the
body is eternal . . .   The Bhagavad Gita

*H*ugh Lynn Cayce said that he lived in a household
where the paranormal world of psychic phenomena was a normal part of day-to-day living. Hugh Lynn
and his younger brother, Edgar Evans, grew up in an environment where their father's daily psychic reading sessions were an ordinary part of life.

"I thought everybody's father gave readings," Edgar
Evans said, laughing. "I thought everybody talked about
dreams over breakfast. I learned very quickly—as I got

older—that this wasn't the case."[1]

"Day-to-day living with my father, Edgar Cayce, was an adventure in psychic experience," Hugh Lynn said. "I never knew what was going to happen next, what he was going to say, or what unusual thing was going to take place right in the middle of the house. Many fascinating experiences happened to him while he was unconscious during the readings sessions, and many happened while he was awake."[2]

In many ways, the Cayce family had a unique "insider's view" of the unseen worlds, through the experiences Edgar Cayce discussed and shared with his family, especially those concerning the soul's survival after physical death. Hugh Lynn and Edgar Evans grew up *knowing* that death was simply a journey to a higher level of consciousness.

"Living with my father, listening to his stories," Hugh Lynn added, "and having my own experiences helped me to understand the deeper meaning of life and the dimensions of consciousness we pass to after death."[3]

One of Hugh Lynn's most vivid memories of such experiences happened with his deceased grandfather, L.B. Cayce.

"My grandfather came back to our house after his death," he said. "He had been buried in Hopkinsville, Kentucky, and several days later he showed up in Virginia Beach. All of us in the house could hear him, but we couldn't see him. My father, Gladys Davis [Edgar Cayce's readings stenographer], my brother, even the postman experienced this phenomenon."[4]

The patriarch of the Cayce family died rather unexpectedly while visiting family in Hopkinsville:

> He had gone on a visit to see my aunt and there he died. My father went to the funeral. The rest of

the family didn't go, and about three days after my
father returned to Virginia Beach, my grandfather
showed up. Everybody in our house could hear him.
My father insisted that [my grandfather] was "straight-
ening out his papers," and that he was going on very
soon, but that he had left some things undone—he
hadn't planned on dying. I could not believe he was
there—I thought it must be a rat, or the floor set-
tling, or something making those noises. I kept running upstairs but couldn't see anything. I even
grabbed the postman one day as he was delivering
mail at the front door, and he knew my grandfather,
used to talk to him, and I dragged him on inside the
door and I said, "Listen, and you tell me what you
hear!" And he listened and upstairs you could hear
[my grandfather] moving around in his room. And
the postman said, "What in the world? Is somebody
up there?" And I told him it was my grandfather up
there. And he turned the color of a sheet and left—
and he delivered the mail from the gate from then
on! He wouldn't even come into the yard. You could
hear this strange phenomenon of this man being
there; we even heard breathing. This all happened
during lunchtime with my father there, my mother,
my brother—all of us heard it. "He won't be here
long," my father said, "just leave him alone and let
him get straightened out. He's all right. You can pray
for him if you want, but don't bother him anymore."
I got up from the table and told [Edgar Cayce] that I
was going to go upstairs and look again. "If I were
you, I wouldn't do that," Dad said. But I didn't listen, and this time I didn't make it all the way upstairs. I got to the landing. And I ran into my
grandfather. I ran *through* him in a way—and it was
cold. Seeing him, *knowing* it was he, scared the day-

lights out of me. Every hair on my head stood straight up in the air—I felt as if I'd received an electrical shock of some sort.[5]

Hugh Lynn deduced from this experience—and many other encounters he had throughout his lifetime—that there are many stages to the death transition, just as there are many stages of growth in the physical world:

Time doesn't seem to matter much there on the other side. We don't just die and that's it. It seems that we gradually leave this world and move on. Like my grandfather—he was taking care of some business still left here, and he'd be ready to move on. Some souls move on more quickly than others—just as some children develop and grow faster than others in *this* world. The transition we call death is really a birth, and it's a matter of soul development how quickly we become self-aware.[6]

The Cayce readings spell out clearly that death is as natural as birth—perhaps more so, in many ways. One interesting passage says it is easier to leave this physical world than it is to be born into it. Another says it happens so easily, we may not even realize it:

There are many experiences in a life's journey in the earth that are much more serious than that man calls death . . . 5195-1

Death—as commonly spoken of—is only passing through God's other door . . . As to how long [before the soul becomes self-aware]—many an individual has remained in that [state] called death for . . . *years* without realizing it was dead! 1472-2

Rather than asking ourselves, "Does the soul survive physical death?" we would do well to ask ourselves, "How quickly will I 'wake up' to my environment after death and become conscious?"

Hugh Lynn believed that by working with dreams and meditation we can gain a deeper understanding of the realms after death and prepare for the journey:

A third of our physical lives is spent in an altered state of consciousness—in sleep. With this simile, then, we have a way of understanding the transition we call death. If you don't have any other reason for recording your dreams, you should write them [down] to find out what kind of place you're going to go when you die. Dreams provide a map of the realms *you are creating*—of where you'll go after death. You can begin to understand from your dreams what it's like there.[7]

Edgar Cayce's readings indicate that, during sleep, the sixth sense is very active and the soul is more "awake" than while in physical consciousness:

. . . sleep is a shadow of, that intermission in earth's experience of, that state called death . . .
. . . this, then—the sixth sense, as it be termed for consideration here, partakes of the *accompanying* entity that is ever on guard before the throne of the Creator itself . . . 5754-1

The only difference between sleep and death is that we return to the body after a period of sleep. At physical death, we remain in the realms of the spirit:

There has been, and ever when the physical consciousness is at rest, the other self communes with the *soul* of the body, see? or it goes *out* into that realm of experience in the relationships of all experiences of that entity that may have been throughout the *eons* of time . . .

Hence through such an association in sleep there may have come that peace, that understanding, that is accorded by that which has been correlated through that passage of the selves of a body in sleep. 5754-2

During Hugh Lynn's freshman year at Washington and Lee University, he had an experience during which he came to a deeper understanding of this concept. A college friend was killed in an automobile accident after leaving a fraternity party at Natural Bridge in Lexington, Virginia. Hugh Lynn recounted a dream experience in which he believed he communicated with his friend, Gus Elias, just after his death:

It was a strange experience. Sometime in the middle of that night, I awoke suddenly and sat up in bed. A peculiar thing was happening: I was sitting up, but my body was lying down! I became aware that I could move away from my body by simply choosing to do so. I was experimenting with this moving about outside of the body when the room suddenly began to fill up with a form that looked like a cloud. It was absolutely dark, but I could easily see the whole room. I focused my attention on the cloud, and out of it came a hand and I heard a voice—shouting very excitedly. 'Cayce, Cayce! Come up here! This is terrific! I've got to show you!' It was Gus's voice. I could see his hand clearly, beckoning me. Still out of body, I moved from the floor up to the cloud. As I touched it, I was suddenly very afraid. Just as quickly, I was back in my physical body, back to waking consciousness, sitting up in bed. I was trying to figure out what kind of crazy dream I'd had.[8]

Hugh Lynn learned very quickly this was no ordinary dream. Shortly after this unusual experience, someone began pounding on his dorm room door:

> Someone said, "Cayce, get up! Gus Elias was killed at midnight. They're bringing his body in!" As it turned out, Gus had been killed in an auto accident coming back from a party at Natural Bridge. He was thrown from the rumble seat, killed instantly from a skull fracture. At that point, the dream made complete sense: It wasn't a dream at all. I was able to experience Gus making his transition   because the sleep state of consciousness is the same as the consciousness we *pass to upon physical death*.[9]

The ability to communicate with the dead through our dreams *and* in the waking state is dependent upon our ability to shift our consciousness. Hugh Lynn's experience with Gus Elias is a good illustration: Because he was already in an altered state of consciousness—sleep—Hugh Lynn was able to link up on a mental and spiritual level with the subconscious mind of his friend. Thousands of people have reported vivid dream experiences soon after the death of a loved one. In many cases, *these encounters seem more vivid than their usual dreams*. In light of the Cayce readings' view of the continuity of life, such dreams are not simply illusions of wish fulfillment brought about by bereavement; it is just as natural to communicate during the dream state with our loved ones who have died as it is to communicate with them over the telephone or in person. Just as there are many avenues through which we can communicate with one another here in the physical world (via telephone, mail, the Internet, and, of course, person to person) there exist "unseen avenues" through which we can contact our loved ones after death. Hugh Lynn added:

> We travel through dimensions and planes of consciousness during the time we sleep and we prepare for where we're going after death.[10]

It is natural, then, that we would have numerous encounters with deceased loved ones through and during the dream state. People who had dreamed of their dead husbands, wives, and parents came to Edgar Cayce. Most of them were pleasantly startled by what Cayce told them in their readings: Dream encounters with the dead *are real* communications with the other side. These fascinating readings are an important facet in understanding the nature of death, dying, and the realms of consciousness after physical death.

A thirty-nine-year-old woman (reading 3416-1) came to Edgar Cayce after the death of her brother. She had experienced vivid dream and waking encounters in which she seemed to be in communication with him:

"The entity has had the experience of awaking at night and feeling the presence of her brother," Gertrude said, reading the woman's question. "Would appreciate an explanation of this."

"This is a reality," Cayce answered.

"On June 2, 1942, the entity heard her brother calling her—was this the exact time that he passed on?"

"Not the exact time," Cayce replied, "but when the entity could—and found the attunement such as to speak with thee."

"Was there something he wanted her to know?"

"Much that he needs of thee. Forget not to pray for and with him; not seeking to hold him but that he, too, may walk the way to the Light, in and through the experience. For this is well. Those who have passed on need the prayers of those who live aright. For the prayers of those who would be righteous in spirit may save many who have erred, even in the flesh." (3416-1)

Hugh Lynn Cayce told many people at his lectures that the intellectual conscious mind is not capable of fully understanding the experiences after death because we're dealing with *fourth*-dimensional experiences that far transcend reason, intellect, and linear thought. We will rest easy and understand fully the nature of death and dying only by setting aside the usual mode of rational thinking and entering into a deeper state of consciousness, such as meditation or deep prayer. The mind then enters the fourth dimension of thought and feeling, and it is at that deep level that knowledge and understanding of death and dying are realized—and the realization is far beyond words or reasoning.

"You can drive yourself crazy trying to use the three-dimensional mind in an attempt to understand fourth-dimensional experiences," Hugh Lynn said. "It doesn't work. Until you enter within. There, according to the readings, a deeper, soul-level understanding and *knowing* that death is only an illusion will be understood and realized."[11]

Adeline Blumenthal, the wife of one of Edgar Cayce's financial supporters during the 1920s, came to understand this principle in a dramatic and inspiring manner. She had many readings from Edgar Cayce on health and spiritual matters. She came to Cayce one particular day because she had been dreaming of her dead mother and of a family friend who had also died rather unexpectedly. Adeline submitted questions to be asked to the entranced Cayce:

(Q) [I dreamt I] heard a voice that I recognized as J.S.'s . . . who loved me dearly as a child, yet whom I have not seen in 2 to 3 years. The impression of J.S. talking to me was very pronounced . . . I felt that she was there as [Mother's] transition was made—was now with Mother as she said to me: *"Your mother is as happy as ever . . . "* Recall and explain to me please.

Once again, Edgar Cayce was able to attune to the realms of higher knowledge and offer inspiring and comforting guidance to a bereaved daughter:

(A) In this there is given to the entity that understanding of what is meant by the life other than the physical. For, as it is seen that the companionship of loved ones seek the companionship in that plane . . . there is seen the message coming from the loved one [J.S.] to the one regarding the loved one, showing then that companionship.
    . . . the entity should . . . know that the mother lives in that realm in which there is recognized J.S., and that the companionship is there . . . For those many changes must come to each and every entity in its development. And as these are seen, then, the strength, the understanding should be gained by this entity. For . . . she [the mother] is *well, happy,* and *free* from the care as is given in the earth's plane . . .
    (Q) J.S. . . . died 3 weeks before Mother—how and

why did this entity transmit the message to me?

(A) . . . The entity may answer same from within self, if the entity would not condemn self for physical conditions [surrounding the mother's death], for this brings the sorrow in the heart . . . Then, when this is laid aside, there may be seen how that the friendship, the love of one close, near and dear, is ready to give that aid . . . For, as is seen then in this [dream] presented . . . *not alone* does the mother go out; not alone in that unseen world, yet with that same care, that same love, raised to a better *understanding* . . .

(Q) Then, does one spirit guide another over?

(A) Lo! I am with thee, and though I walk through the valley of the shadow of death, my spirit shall guide thee.

(Q) [I heard a] Voice [say]: "Your mother is alive and happy."

(A) Your mother is alive and happy . . . for there is no death, only the transition from the physical to the spiritual plane. Then, as the birth into the physical is given as the time of the new life, just so, then, in physical is the birth into the spiritual.

(Q) Then, does my mother see me and love me as ever?

(A) Sees thee and loves thee as ever. Just as those forces were manifest in the physical world, and the entity entertains and desires and places self in that attunement with those desires of that entity, the love exists . . . for the *soul* liveth and is at peace . . .

As the spirit of self gives that attunement that may be at a oneness with those spirits in that [after-death] sphere, they may know, they may understand, they may gather, that *truth* that *makes* one free. 136-33

Adeline had another dramatic encounter with her mother, and this time she saw her consciously—not in a dream. Adeline's mother had died shortly before Adeline gave birth to her son. The labor was long and difficult. Adeline's husband, Morton, was at her bedside, and she suddenly grabbed his arm and pointed to a corner of the room.

"My mother is with me," Adeline said. "See, she is right there! I can see her!" Adeline had sensed the presence of her mother hovering nearby for the duration of her labor. She felt as if her mother were giving her encouragement and strength throughout the day. Although she had felt her presence, Adeline hadn't consciously *seen* her mother until that moment just before giving birth to a son.

Adeline and Morton came to Edgar Cayce to obtain a reading to help clarify the phenomenal experience. They wrote out the suggestion that would be read to Edgar Cayce as he entered the unconscious state:

GC [Gertrude Cayce]: You will have before you the bodies and the enquiring minds of [Morton] and [Adeline Blumenthal], and the experience they had on the 4th day of April, 1927, in Women's Hospital . . . New York City, with [Adeline] and [Morton Blumenthal] alone in the room and the spirit mother, [Mrs. Levy]. You will give the interpretation and the lesson to be gained by these individuals from this wonderful experience.

EC [Edgar Cayce]: Yes, we have the experience here, and this . . . is but another experience in the lives of these individuals, who are gaining a more vivid and a broader understanding of the oneness of the universal forces . . .

In the experiences as are seen by these entities,

there is gained that knowledge of the fullness of life
. . . for . . . "Lo, I am with you, even unto the end of
the world." . . . For the way that leads to the more
perfect understanding of life is that which leads
into the valley of the shadow of the borderland—
for, as is seen, the borderland is crossed by both [the
living and the deceased] . . .
    And the willingness of the mother is to ever be
present in the mental attitude of the entity, to shield
every thought, every care . . . 136-59

At this point of the reading, Adeline's mother gave a
direct message through Cayce, to both Morton and his
wife, explaining the reason for her manifestation:

> "To [Adeline] I have come, in that certain way
> that makes known the life after death . . . Be thou
> faithful, then, in those lessons I have given to you,
> to [Morton], and to the baby—who comes from
> among us, and whom I have known before." [The
> quote marks apparently indicated a direct message
> from the mother.]

Edgar Cayce intimated in this reading that our loved
ones can become guardian angels after death, reassuring us with their presence and, as the Blumenthals experienced, being with us at times of great crisis and great
joy.
    A fifty-seven-year-old woman came to Cayce to ask
him questions regarding her dead father, whom she had
sensed around the family on several occasions.
    "Does the spirit of my father ever hover around his
family . . . ?" the woman asked.
    "Oft," Cayce replied, "as the self has felt that abiding
strength, through those periods when there seemed no

end to the discontent as about self, does the body know and feel that spirit guiding, aiding, strengthening; for, as He has given, 'He will give his angels charge concerning thee, lest thou unwittingly dash thy foot against a stone.'" (2118-1)

In July 1934, Edgar Cayce had a strange experience while giving reading 5756-13, in which he seemed to be communicating with deceased family members. The transcribed reading appears as a one-sided conversation—as if Edgar Cayce was talking on a telephone and only one side was overheard. This experience occurred after completing a routine series of physical readings.

"We are through for the present," Cayce said, indicating the reading session was complete.

Gertrude began to read the usual posthypnotic suggestion which would bring her husband back from the deep trance to waking consciousness. "Now, all the organs of the body are functioning properly," Gertrude said, "and in two minutes, Edgar Cayce will awaken normally—"

"There are some here that would speak with those that are present," Cayce interrupted, "if they desire to so communicate with them."

Gertrude and Gladys Davis looked at each other in surprise. They had learned from past experience that some message of importance was sometimes given when Edgar Cayce ignored the waking suggestion.

"We desire to have at this time that which would be given," Gertrude replied.

There was a long pause. Edgar Cayce lay sleeping on the couch. Gladys sat very still with her steno pad, waiting to transcribe in shorthand the message to follow. She and Gertrude silently wondered who the entities were that "would speak with those present." Cayce exclaimed, as if he were trying to quiet a room full of people:

Don't speak all at once! Yes. I knew you would be waiting, though. Yes? Haven't found him before? All together then now, huh? . . . *Who?* Dr. House? No. Oh, no. No, she is alright. Yes, *lots* better. Isn't giving any trouble now. Haven't seen her? Why? Where have you been? Oh. She is in another change? How long will they stay there? Oh, they don't count time like that. Oh, you do have 'em. Well, those must be pretty now, if they are all growing like that way. Yes? Yes, I'll tell her about 'em. Tell Gertrude you are all together now, huh? Uncle Porter, Dr. House, your mother? And Grandma. Oh, Grandpa still building. Oh, he made the house; yeah. Tell Tommy what? *Yes!* Lynn? Yes, he's at home. Oh, you knew that! Huh? Ain't any difference? Well, how about the weather? Oh, the weather don't affect you now. Don't change. Oh, you have what you want to—depends on where you go. Sure, when you are subject to that anyway. Little baby too! How big is it? Oh, he's *grown* now, huh? Yes. Coming back! When? Oh. Uh-huh. Alright. Why? Oh yes, they hear you—I'm sure they do. I hear you! For Gertrude? Yes, she is here—she hears you. Oh, yes!

GC: I don't hear. May I have the message?

EC: Sure, she hears you. Don't you hear her talking? No, I don't know what she says.

GC: I don't hear. Will you repeat the message for me?

At that point, it was as if Edgar Cayce handed the "telephone" to the deceased family member whom he had been conversing with, and stepped aside. Cayce then became a medium for that person:

Mama and Dr. House and Uncle Porter and the

baby—we are all here. Grandpa has built the home here, and it's *nice!* And we are all waiting until you come, and we will all be here ready—we are getting alone *fine,* doing *well,* yes. No. No more troubles now, for spring borders [?] all along the way; for we have reached together where we see the light and know the pathway to the Savior is along the narrow way that leads to *His* throne. We are on that plane where you have heard it spoken of that the body, the mind, are one with those things we have builded. Yes, I still play baseball and Charlie has recently joined my club and I am still Captain to many of 'em. Well, we will be waiting for you! 5756-13

At that point, Edgar Cayce became silent, and Gertrude again read the waking suggestion. Both Gladys and Gertrude sat in astonishment as they waited for Edgar to awaken. The unusual one-sided conversation seemed to come from an entire of group of Gertrude's deceased family members. Even before they sought a reading to clarify the after-death communication, Gertrude was certain that a major part of the message was conveyed through her husband from her younger brother, Charlie, who had died years earlier of tuberculosis.

Hugh Lynn explained:

My father would now and then stop and talk to people along the way back after giving a reading. He would talk to people, *dead people,* after the reading was stopped and he was returning. These instances reveal a great deal about the nature of life after death. Evidently, he stopped on the way back from the level of attunement from which the reading was given. He recognized several individuals who wished to communicate and began a conver-

sation with them. Those present in the room could
hear only one side of the conversation. Gertrude's
brother, who died years earlier of tuberculosis, had
been forced to give up [playing baseball] during the
last years of his life. Evidently, he was able to continue this activity, [based on the comment], "I still
play baseball."

This brother also speaks of a home that had been
built by my great grandfather. He hadn't finished his
house when he died—he was an architect. He finished the house, apparently, on the other side. It
became a place where those who, from this large
family, kept coming and stopping, and taking off
from there to other levels and other planes. And he
[the brother] described what he had been doing
[playing baseball, etc.] and then talked about getting ready to move on into other planes of consciousness. Our loved ones are very close to us after
death.[12]

Cayce's readings indicate that our relationships with
our loved ones in the earth are "reflections" or "shadows"
of the *real spiritual relationships that exist in the spiritual worlds.* The love that brings us together in this world
cannot be seen as a tangible *thing,* but it is clearly felt,
experienced, and treasured within us. It is as real as a
physical object. This common bond of love that carries
us through our lives and relationships far surpasses and
transcends time, space, and the illusion of death. If all
things in our finite physical world are but shadows of the
real spiritual world, then what a great event it must be
for the soul to move beyond the shadow of life, into the
realms where the Source of all life emanates in all its fullness and splendor, no longer hindered by the limitations
of a physical body or material world. As we ponder the

eternal essence of love and the continuity of life, we can begin to see why Gertrude Cayce's deceased brother was so joyous and enthusiastic in his message through the reading: "We'll all be waiting for you." The souls who have passed through the doorway called death are no longer hindered by the limitations of a physical body. Is it any wonder those speaking to Cayce were anxious for the Cayce family to "come home"? When we physically die, it is like a homecoming to those on the other side whom we've known and loved. It is not a traumatic, frightening experience for the person who dies. The soul is immediately in the care and companionship of other souls it has known—and there is great peace and illumination, just as there is great peace and serenity surrounding a newborn baby.

Because so many of the Cayce family members seemed to be "present" during that unusual reading, Edgar and Gertrude sought more information through the readings on how and why such phenomena occurred. On July 17, 1934, the reading period was set aside to answer just those questions.

After Edgar Cayce was comfortably situated in the reading room, and he entered into the sleep-like state, Gertrude read the suggestion for the psychic reading:

GC: You will have before you the body and enquiring mind of Edgar Cayce and all present in this room, in regard to the experience following the reading Monday afternoon, July 9, 1934; explaining to us what happened—and why—at that particular time, answering the question that may be asked.

EC: Yes, we have the body, the enquiring mind, Edgar Cayce, and those present in this room, together with the experience had by all present in the room on July 9, 1934 . . .

Here we find, in the experience, that there were
those [present] that were in attune . . . and these
[entities] sought . . . to communicate of themselves
that there might be known . . . their *continued
existence in a world of matter but of finer matter . . .*
and they sought through those channels . . . the
soul-force of the body [Edgar Cayce] was passing at
the particular time . . . that which would *make
known their presence in activity* [author's italics].
5756-14

The Cayce family was very happy to receive news from
their deceased relatives through the readings, but to the
waking Edgar Cayce, it was both a reassurance and a be-
wildering experience for him, since he had no conscious
recall of anything he said while giving the readings. The following reading on the subject of spirit communication
was requested by Edgar Cayce himself to further shed
light on how such after-life messages came through
him:

. . . the various communications given at the time
were from those thought to be dead (from the
physical viewpoint) . . . yet their souls, their person-
alities, their individualities, live on . . . Hence communicated, as heard, through the soul forces of the
body Edgar Cayce . . . In this vision there enters
many of those conditions that, to the material
mind, are hard to be understood . . . For, as it is seen,
in that realm of the spiritual world there is the peace
and communion of loved ones, in and from the
earth's plane. Chaos does not rule, but rather that
of oneness of purpose and truth. And when such
unions, when such meetings, come in accord with
conditions being viewed in the material world,

these same influences come to assist, when allowed to, in the material plane. For, as is seen, there is given the compass to the physical being to guide him in the material condition of life. 294-74

Hugh Lynn described a strange experience where his father was told that Edgar's mother was about to die. The message was given at the close of one of his psychic readings. After Edgar Cayce woke up, Gladys and Gertrude relayed the unsettling message. Edgar left Virginia Beach for Hopkinsville, Kentucky, that evening:

> The reading on my grandmother said that she wasn't seriously ill, but it told my father if he wanted to see her alive, he should go to her immediately. Dad went to Hopkinsville and walked in on his mother unexpectedly. She met him at the door and she seemed perfectly all right. The next day she went to bed, and the day after that she died. Very calmly, very quietly, without any problem. No suffering. And my father sat there beside her and talked to her. She was very "in and out" and then he began to see and talk to her mother and father. And he watched his mother talk to them as he sat by her bedside. And then she passed.[13]

These conscious and unconscious experiences of the Cayce family shed a great deal of light upon all of our experiences. To many people who sought out Edgar Cayce, trying to understand the continuity of the soul's existence, a recurrent precept was given by Cayce in many ways, for many people. The essence of his answers was this:

You are not a physical being with a spiritual being in-

side. You are a spiritual being who—for a short time—re-
sides in a body. You do not "have" a soul. You are *a soul.*
You are not *the body.*

The Cayce readings frequently stated that in the spiritual dimensions, time does not exist; it is only valid in
third-dimensional reality—the material realms. All is at
at-onement. Time is a dimension that the soul passes
through that it may awaken to know the true relationship it has with the Creator. The soul enters at birth into
a limited space-time continuum to learn lessons in the
finite, material world. The most important lessons—our
ability to love, to forgive, to grow in patience and grace—
all acted out in the framework of daily life, working and
personal relationships, etc.—*go with the soul after physi-*
cal death. These lessons are not physical. They are spiritual lessons enacted in the physical world.

In this light, we can see how our ability to love or not
to love creates the very fabric of our after-death environment. In short, we create heaven or hell for ourselves,
based upon our application of spiritual laws during
earthly life.

If the earthly life has been lived as a quest solely for
power, then regardless of other soul growth and development, universal law requires that after death, the soul
will be held in an earthbound state of consciousness focused upon the earth but not in it, surrounded by the
thoughts, desires, and feelings for power that the soul
loved in the earth. This is a transitional experience, to be
sure—but time there is not the same as here in the three-
dimensional world.

By the same token, if we choose to hold in mind a
spiritual ideal that helps us grow in awareness, one that
helps us forgive others and love more deeply at the end
of the physical life, the great light of unconditional love

will guide us to the realms of peace, serenity, and higher heavenly states of consciousness. Where we go after death is dependent upon the choices we make during our physical life.

One of the most reassuring truths found in Cayce's readings is the statement that *we do not pass through the death transition alone.* We don't leave this world alone any more than we enter it alone, and leaving this world, according to the readings, is much easier than entering it. What we term "death" is actually a return to a broader, more expansive consciousness where the soul is free from the limitations of physical form. Perhaps this is the reason the thousands of people who have had near-death experiences report feeling *more alive and more awake* than during their physical lives. The unseen realm is the true home of the soul; the earth is a necessary school for learning and growth. It is a brief interim in the scheme of eternity—an important interim, nonetheless—but physical death is, in many ways, a return "home" with new lessons learned. In the return to the realm, not of darkness and death, but of true light and living, we gather together with loved ones and those souls of like mind, just as we gather with friends and family during our physical lives.

6

Case Studies of
After-Death Communication

*E*dgar Cayce's readings compared the transition at death to moving from one town or city to another. Although we may travel far distances in this world, we still maintain communication with people through the telephone, letters, the Internet, etc. Just so, there are ways and means that the living can communicate with souls in other dimensions of consciousness.

An interesting question was posed to Cayce regarding communication with the dead while in trance:

(Q) Is it possible for this body, Edgar Cayce in this [trance] state, to communicate with anyone who has passed into the spirit world?

(A) The spirit of all that have passed from the physical plane remain about the plane until their development carry them onward or are returned for their development here [earth plane]. When they are in the plane of communication or remain within this sphere, any may be communicated with. *There are thousands about us here at present.* [author's italics] 3744-1

There are times when it is easier than others for the dead to communicate with the living. The optimum state of consciousness to have a visitation with the deceased is in dreams or in the "in-between state" of consciousness between waking and sleep, sometimes referred to as the *hypnagogic* state of consciousness. It is in this state that our souls are most receptive to the realms where the deceased reside, due to the "network" of the collective unconsciousness of all people.

It isn't uncommon for the deceased to *appear* to the living shortly after death and communicate in some form. These apparitions take on many forms and may be seen during the waking state of consciousness, in dreams, or during periods of deep meditation. In many instances the dead will "speak" through circumstances, coincidences, or occurrences where a "trademark" of the deceased is manifested for the bereaved. At times, the soul attempts communication to lend comfort to the bereaved; in other instances it is the *soul* who needs guidance and assistance from the living, as we've seen in previous chapters. In *Testimony of Light,* Frances Banks detailed how such communications occur between the living and the dead:

There are Stations on this plane where communication with the earth plane is possible.[1]

In these Stations there are helpers and servers

who have dedicated their knowledge and service to helping those who long to send messages to loved ones still on earth. The technique employed, I understand, is quite "special" and very difficult at first to follow, even by those who desire to use it. But there *are* Stations, there are Directors for this work, there are administrators and (in a sense) technicians to run them . . . [2]

. . . For on this telepathic wave I can write with you these scraps of information on the all-controversial subject of Life After Death . . . but now I am at liberty to tell you that this is not a solo performance on my part . . . There is a Band who help and guide me in the selection of incidents to be telepathed to you . . . there are others in the Band, and I understand that we are merely instruments in this work. *The veil between the worlds must be rent asunder . . . People living on earth, the erudite, the cultured and clever minds, as well as the devotional and religious minds, and the uneducated, the illiterate and the closed minds must all be reached. All need this knowledge to remove fear which is one of the darkest and most powerful earth-emotions which has to be fought and conquered before peace and progress can come to the earth.*[3] [author's italics]

Edgar Cayce Helps a Deceased Soul to the Light

Hugh Lynn Cayce recounted a story in which his father had an unusual after-death encounter with a woman he had known during his early career as a photographer. The woman had died relatively young in life and visited Edgar Cayce some years later at his home in Virginia Beach:

One morning he woke up all excited with this very interesting and strange story. He had been asleep the night before, he said, and there had been a tapping on the window. He became aware of someone out there talking to him and he recognized who it was. It was a girl who had worked for him in his studio in Selma, Alabama, many years before. And he knew she was dead. But she was a very proper young lady and she was asking him to please come down and let her in at the front door; she wanted to see him but she wanted to come in the proper manner. He went down and opened the door, and she was standing there. He could see through her, but she was solid enough to come in and sit down and talk to him. She wanted to know what to do.

"I know I am dead," she said. "I've been living with my mother and father. They keep running off and leaving me, and I don't know where to go or what to do. I was around the [photography] studio and I remembered if I could just get to you, you could tell me what do. I've had an awful time."[4]

The next part of the story illustrates the holding power of our belief systems and the unusual circumstances the soul can find itself surrounded by after physical death:

"You know, I died of that illness that I had, the stomach trouble," the woman explained. "The doctor operated on me and I died during the operation. When I got over to this side, I was still sick, still suffering, and I was very concerned. Then the doctor died and he finished the operation on this side. I'm all right now."[5]

Hugh Lynn said that it had been many years since she had died, but she was unaware of the passage of time:

Years had passed, but it seemed like ten minutes to her . . . So Dad told her about the light, how to look for it and how to pray about it. He said that he would pray for her and have the [healing prayer] group pray for her, and that when she saw this light, she should follow it; then she'd know where to go. You hear us mention every once in a while about a light that comes in meditation. And we'd better find it before we move on to the other side. We may need it, to find where to go. Because of the timelessness found on the other side, a lost feeling can be very disturbing. So we need to be able to move.[6]

A Murdered Woman Returns to Her Son

When Jay[7] was fourteen years old, his mother disappeared and was never found. He believes that she was abducted and killed over a drug deal. She had been battling a heroin addiction off and on all of Jay's life. In the years of her addiction, she came to know well the drug underworld and some rather dangerous people. Jay remained close to his mother, even through the darker periods of her life when the addiction took its toll and she resorted to prostitution to support her habit.

"No matter how bad off she was," Jay said, "she always made sure I had enough food to eat. She always made sure I was safe. We were very close."[8]

Six weeks after her disappearance, Jay had a vivid dream of his mother in which he believed she communicated with him. In the dream, he was driving on an isolated highway and crossed over a rusty railroad bridge. Immediately after crossing the bridge, he saw an apparition of his mother.

"She appeared to be dismembered," Jay said, "but not in a grisly way. There were spaces on her body that separated her head from her torso, her arms appeared separated from her shoulders, and I couldn't see her legs. Her face was very clear and her expression was something like, 'pay attention . . . this is very important for you to understand.'"

In the dream, he followed his mother some twenty-five yards from the bridge, through the woods into a small clearing. As they traveled to this clearing, the sun burst through the clouds and the entire scene was illumined. His mother pointed toward the ground. When Jay looked, he immediately knew he was looking at a shallow open grave. Surprisingly, neither Jay nor his mother were distraught in the dream. He was filled with a paradoxical sense of relief as he looked at his mother and at the shallow grave. When he awoke suddenly from the dream, Jay said he was filled with a "knowing" about two things simultaneously: He knew his mother was dead and that her soul was all right.

"I knew in some way that she had been killed," Jay said. "And strange as it sounds, when I awoke I was filled with a great sense of peace as this understanding came to me. I felt my mother's sense of relief just at *my knowing and understanding what had happened to her.*"[9] [author's italics]

Thomson J. Hudson's exhaustive book, *The Law of Psychic Phenomena,* illustrated a case that uncannily echoes Jay's dream encounter with his dead mother:

> The character of the manifestation [appearance of the deceased] is as varied as are the phases of human emotion or the objects of human desire . . . When a mother dies at a distance from her children, she is often filled with an intense longing to see them once more before she passes away. The result often is that she projects a phantasm into their

presence which takes a lingering look into the faces
of the loved ones, and then fades away.

All phantasms of the dead are those who have
died under circumstances of great mental stress or
emotion . . . [A] murdered man feels, at the supreme
moment, an intense longing to acquaint the world
with the circumstances of his "taking off"; and he
conceives the thought of reproducing the scene on
the spot until its significance is understood and the
murderer is brought to justice . . . those [of the liv-
ing] whose nerves are strong enough to withstand
the shock may nightly witness a realistic reproduc-
tion of the tragedy. This may continue for days,
months, or even years, but invariably ceases when
the object is accomplished . . . [10]

In the case of Jay, his mother appeared in order to let
her child know that she had not run away of her own vo-
lition, but that she had been victimized and could not
physically return to him. The evidence that this was his
dead mother's desire was the immense state of peace
that Jay felt in the dream. The dream repeated itself over
the course of seven nights. After each subsequent night,
Jay's sense of peace increased, and his grief subsided.
After the seventh night, the dream encounters with his
mother ended—so did the paralyzing grief he had experienced for the six weeks prior. Jay has not yet found the
railroad bridge or the clearing where his mother showed
him her grave in the dream. But he feels certain that the
dream encounter with his mother was a real experience
that enabled her to rest after her brutal death and enabled him to go on with his life, knowing that death was
not the end.

A Drowned Girl Communicates

Edgar Cayce experienced a similar situation when he and his wife, Gertrude, sat down to experiment with a Ouija board in the early 1930s. Cayce reported that a message came through the board from a little girl who had drowned in a lake:

> [I] Have seen several expressions of the Ouija Board that were most remarkable . . . one evening saw several messages given that all proved to be absolutely true tho [sic] it was impossible for any one in that room to have known any thing of either of the messages received—or of the people they were purported to be from or to whom they were addressed—yet the address of each one given proved correct—and the message helpful to the person to whom it was sent—for instance one of the messages was: "I am a little girl named B.R. . . . please let my Father D.R. . . . know I did not run away from home, but was drowned in the log pond[;] my father runs a saw mill—tell him to please get my bones from such and such place in the pond . . . " The father was written to—he had lost a little girl and found her bones where it was said he would find them. That would be positive proof to many . . . 1196-1, Reports

In this instance, the immense grief of her father was directly communicated to the little girl on the other side. Naturally, this prompted the soul of the child to seek to communicate through any open channel. The Ouija board, with Edgar Cayce as one of its operators, represented that open channel through which the spirit could communicate from the other side. For the child, alleviating the grief of her father was necessary before she could move on to higher realms in the afterlife.

Many strange phenomena can surround the death of loved ones, more times than not, breaking through the barrier between the worlds of the living and the dead. Hudson described a theory in *The Law of Psychic Phenomena* that defines this experience, particularly in cases where death was sudden or violent:

> The generally accepted theory which has been employed to account for this coincidence is that the soul, thus torn suddenly and prematurely from the body, retains more of the material elements of the body than it does when death is the result of gradual disintegration and the natural separation of the material from the immaterial. It is thought that the physical elements thus retained temporarily by the spirit enable it to make itself visible to the living as well as perform certain feats of physical strength attributed to some spirits. This is very plausible at first glance, and in the absence of any facts to the contrary might be accepted as the true theory ... [11]

A Telephone Call from Beyond

In many instances, souls on the other side will communicate to the living in an intangible way, without actually appearing in a dream or vision. The following two cases illustrate that some after-death communications are conveyed through signs and circumstances that bear the "trademark" of the deceased personality, even down to the departed's sense of humor.

Barbara[12] nursed her husband through the final stages of terminal bone cancer. Their marriage had been a happy one, filled with much laughter and humor. For as long as Barbara could remember, her husband had been a whistler. He not only whistled while he worked, but he also whistled when he was puttering about the house.

"He drove the family crazy with his whistling," Barbara remembered, laughing. "But it wasn't annoying so much as it was just *him*. It was part of his nature. He whistled constantly."

Prior to his death, Barbara's husband laughingly told her he would have to make a tape of his whistling before he died, so she wouldn't miss him so much. They both had a good laugh over that, and the incident was soon forgotten as the ravages of the cancer took their toll. After his death, Barbara was going through the long dark days of grieving, and she missed her husband terribly.

"I had come home and I just broke down," Barbara said. "I was so lost without him and I didn't know how I was going to make it. It was a confusion of emotions—anger, loss, hurt—oh, it was terrible."

Barbara had been out for some time, so she went to the answering machine to retrieve her telephone messages.

"I pushed the button on the answering machine," Barbara said, "and the only message that was on the tape was of someone whistling. It went on and on and then there was only silence. The tape played out until it reached the end."

Barbara sat in shocked silence as the rest of tape played itself out, without any other messages. What is bizarre about this occurrence is that her answering machine is *voice-activated*; when the caller stops talking, it automatically shuts off and rewinds.

Barbara sat in confused silence for a time. Suddenly, she remembered what her husband had said before his death: "I'm going to have to make you a tape of my whistling so you won't miss me so much."

"When he did something, he did it with a flourish,"

Barbara said. "He had a wonderful sense of humor and always had to do things to 'top' himself or others. I don't know how such a thing was possible [the inexplicable whistling on the tape], but that would be *exactly* in his nature to do something like that, something that would make me laugh instead of cry."[13]

It's important to remember that the entirety of our soul and personality carries on after death. The dead may convey a comforting message to the living in the same manner that they would convey such a message during their lives—with their own "trademark" of humor, lightness, and love. According to Edgar Cayce:

> . . . do not consider for a moment that an individual soul-entity passing from an earth plane as a Catholic, a Methodist, an Episcopalian, is something else because he is dead! He's only a dead Episcopalian, Catholic or Methodist. 254-92

A Father Communicates with His Daughters

Janet[14] and her sister received the news of the unexpected death of their father. He had dropped dead of a heart attack at the age of seventy-two. The night after the funeral, Janet dreamed she was sitting in a chair, feeling sad about her father's death.

"I saw him very clearly," Janet said, "and he was as lively as ever. He seemed to be very busy cleaning himself up—it was like he was clearing all of his clogged arteries out. I said, 'Dad, if I had known you needed to do that, I would have suggested taking you to a health center where they do chelation therapy; that way you would have had the help you needed.'"

The father smiled at Janet and said, "No, that's all right. I'm better off dead."

Janet awoke from the dream feeling it was a very real contact. Soon, another communication—this one reflecting her father's sense of humor—occurred that gave pause for thought to the entire family.

"We were all telling stories about Dad one evening," Janet said. "And my uncle told this hilarious story where he and my Dad had gone on this hunting trip, taking the dog with them. As it happened, the dog got sprayed by a skunk not once but *twice* during the trip. Because they were traveling by car, they had no choice but to put the dog in the car, stench or no stench. My dad and my uncle drove all the way home with their heads hung out the window. For weeks after they got back, the smell of the skunk was everywhere, in the car, in their clothes, and of course, on the dog. Well, after that night of story-telling, my sister had prayed for a sign from Dad that he was all right. She missed him terribly, as we all did. Suddenly, the fragrance of a skunk came floating through the window! My sister said something like, 'Dad, is that the sign?' She went outside the house to investigate, to see if a skunk had sprayed nearby. There was no scent of a skunk anywhere. And just as suddenly as the fragrant message came through the window, it was gone."

The sister was astonished by the experience, but they both laughed over the incident. Janet said it was exactly the type of message her father would send them—something that would lift their spirits, make them laugh, and convey the message, "I'm alive and well."

"That would be just like my dad," Janet said, laughing. "He had the funniest sense of humor. And just to make sure the message got through, Dad made sure that *I smelled it too!* [author's italics] It happened several times during our visit, and my sister and I couldn't believe it—but then again, we could! That was just like him."[15]

Just as Barbara had experienced with her husband, Janet

and her sister understood, without question, that their father was happy and as alive as ever on the other side.

A Girl Reassures Friends After Death

Gina had undergone a liver transplant, but the operation was not a success and after several days in a coma, she died. During the coma, Gina's father called Laura, one of the family's close friends, and asked her to pray for Gina so she could make her transition easier.

Laura was terribly upset by the news and went for a long walk, all the while praying and talking to Gina. During her walk, Gina's face appeared to her, looking very troubled. "I don't know what to do," Gina said. Laura felt the right words enter her mind, words that would help her dying friend. She said, "It's okay, Gina, just let go. You'll be fine." Laura clearly saw Gina's face, and after she spoke these few words, Gina appeared calm. The vision disappeared. Laura said this event occurred at approximately 4:00 p.m.

At the time Laura was experiencing this vision, miles away, Gina's sister noticed a dramatic change in her dying sister, who lay in the hospital bed. "Her countenance became peaceful," the sister said. Gina then easily made her transition at 4:25 p.m.

Shortly after her death, Gina's close friend, Mary, was driving to the hospice center where she worked as a volunteer to help children with AIDS. During the drive, Mary suddenly felt Gina's presence in the car. Gina and Mary had met at a conference on spirituality and had become very close friends. They had discussed many topics: spirituality, the possibility of reincarnation, and what happens to the soul after death. Mary had been with Gina and her family up through the time of Gina's transition through death.

"I felt static electricity in the car," Mary said, "like tiny little shocks around my body. I *knew* it was Gina. I felt her with me as I went into [the hospice]. I said aloud, 'Okay, Gina, now you get to meet my kids.' I picked up Johnny, a little boy with AIDS to whom I was very attached. I began telling him a favorite story about angels—that they were always with him, watching over him. I told Johnny that he had a new, very special angel named Gina to watch over him. As soon as I began the story, there was a musical toy rocking horse in the room that began rocking on its own. It continued for ten minutes while I told Johnny about Gina and the angels.

"I knew at the time that it was a sign that Gina was with Johnny and me," Mary said. Johnny passed over in October 1992. I had a sense that between the two of us, we had Johnny covered 'coming and going' and that she would be there to greet him when he passed over."

Mary was more enlightened than surprised by the experience. The two had built a spiritual bond during their brief friendship on earth, and as many people report, Mary wasn't surprised by the phenomenon. Instead, Gina's reassurance filled her with a *knowing* about the continuity of life after death.[16]

Dream Visit to a Dead Friend

Bob[17] had a dream experience in which he communicated with a friend who had died of AIDS-related complications at age twenty-five. Bob had been a hospice volunteer for Mark until the time of Mark's death. Mark assured Bob beforehand that he would try to communicate with Bob after the transition.

"Several years after Mark's death I had a dream in which he appeared in my living room," Bob said. "He was carrying a load of textbooks of some kind. I was startled.

In the dream, I remembered that Mark was dead, and I couldn't believe he was standing in front of me."

In the dream, Bob asked Mark, "What are you doing *here?*" Mark laughed at Bob and responded to his question with a question. "Bob, what are *you* doing *here?*" Momentarily, Bob was disoriented; then he realized he was dreaming and that Mark was communicating with him.

"Mark said, 'Come on, Bob, I'll show you around.' My initial shock was replaced by amazement. I had never had a lucid dream where I *knew* I was dreaming—and here was Mark, looking healthy, vibrant, and fully recovered. He said he would show me around, but that I couldn't take back the memories of what he was going to show me."

Bob remembered only that Mark showed him a large campus and university, similar to what Dr. George Ritchie had seen—a "university of light." There were professors and students walking about—and Mark was right at home with all of them.

"What was so startling to me," Bob added, "was that this place looked exactly like a university campus on earth, only it was brighter, with vivid colors that are difficult to describe. But Mark was still very much in a 'body' and so were all the other souls there. In the midst of all this activity, I asked Mark if he had accomplished everything he wanted to during his life on earth. He smiled at me and said with a great deal of enthusiasm, 'No, I didn't. But I'm taking classes!' Mark pointed at the books he was carrying, and we both laughed. I realized at that moment that the learning and growing indeed continue after death. It was the most vivid dream I've ever had, but I don't believe it was a dream. I was more conscious there in that dream than I've ever been before. When the dream concluded and I said good-bye to Mark,

I returned to waking consciousness like reentering a familiar room; there was no break in consciousness as in normal sleep. It was like I simply changed places or dimensions in an instant."[18]

The way Mark appeared to Bob in the dream is very significant. He appeared healthy, robust, and muscular. People often report the apparitions of deceased loved ones appearing as they did in the prime of their lives. Again, Cayce's readings emphasize that the wasting away of the physical body during a terminal illness does not hinder the soul in any way. The physical passes away; the soul and spiritual forces do not:

> . . . if we learn more and more that separations [at death] are only walking through the rooms as it were of God's house, we become—in these separations, in these experiences—aware of what is meant by that which has been and is the law, as from the beginning, "Know O ye peoples, the Lord thy God is *One!*" And ye must be one—one with one another, one with Him—if ye would be, as indeed ye are, corpuscles in the *life flow* of thy Redeemer! 1391-1

At the point of death, the soul has the choice to let go of its earthly ties and material dimension of consciousness, and to go toward the light for further growth and unfoldment. For some souls, that choice is not obvious; if it has so lived its life on earth in pursuit of the material rather than spiritual unfoldment, the soul can be so wrapped up in its former earthly activity that it may remain in or near the house that it lived in, or near the friends, family, and acquaintances it knew during life, or continue to try to involve itself in the affairs of the living.

The soul's free will continues after death. Each soul is responsible for its own estate here and hereafter. Where the heart's desire is, so does the soul dwell in this world and the next. The less material-minded and more spiritualized the desires and intentions we cultivate, the higher in consciousness we gravitate after death.

A Father Appears to His Daughter After Suicide

Susan[19] and her sisters grew up in a turbulent household with an alcoholic father who was sometimes physically abusive towards them. He ended his own life by shooting himself with a shotgun. In a matter of days after his death, Susan and her sister, June, saw apparitions of their father. Susan dreamed of her father for three successive nights, while June had a waking visionary encounter with him.

Susan was very psychically sensitive and aware, particularly in dream states. Frequently, she had dreams that predicted crises and upheavals. Susan regularly warned her family and close friends of things she had dreamed, and more times than not, the advice was accurate. A number of crisis situations were averted due to her dream guidance. In the dream about her father, Susan noticed that he looked exactly as he had appeared in life.

"Susie, don't tell anyone I'm dead," the father said and vanished.

"It was like he wanted to make what he had done, his suicide, go away," Susan said. "He was fully aware of what he did and knew it was a mistake. I think that's why he told me not to tell anyone." Susan's sister lived on the West Coast at the time of her father's death. Days after his suicide, June saw an apparition of her father sitting on the couch.

"He was talking to her," Susan said, "but she couldn't hear what he said. But he appeared just as he had appeared in life."

Susan was naturally troubled and grief-stricken over her father's death for many years. A close friend introduced to her the idea of communicating with her father via the dream state as a way to have closure and finish up the "unfinished business." Susan missed her father quite badly, and the desire to speak with him was very intense. For two weeks, she worked with a presleep suggestion and held in mind an affirmation that she would communicate with her father in a dream. After two weeks, Susan had a dream experience that startled and amazed her.

"Suddenly in my dream he was standing in front of me, looking irritated," Susan said. "And I was so happy that I finally reached him. I said, 'I have been trying so hard to get a hold of you!'" His response was rather unusual, and he didn't react with the same enthusiasm and happiness that Susan felt.

"He looked at me and said, 'I know! I know! But I'm busy! I've got things to do!'"

Susan felt she had been reprimanded by her father, as if she had interfered with his work on the other side. She had good intentions for wanting to communicate with her father, but apparently her intentions drew him back during a time where he was very involved with his work and study.

"The feeling I had [in the dream]," Susan added, "was similar to the way you would feel if you were trying to keep a guest from leaving your house, when you *knew* they had somewhere else to go. I knew he still loved me and cared for me, and he was fully aware that I had been trying to contact him for weeks. He just had places to go and people to see. I guess I didn't realize how good my communication skills were!"[20]

Susan's experience in receiving an admonishment from her father is reminiscent of a case in the Edgar

Cayce readings. A woman sought answers to questions concerning after-death contact with her late husband:

> (Q) Have I any further contact with my late husband . . . since he has passed on?
> (A) If that is the desire, [he] will continue to hang on . . . Do you wish to call him back to those disturbing forces, or do you wish the self to be poured out for him that he may be happy? Which is it you desire—to satisfy self that you are communicating, or that you are holding him in such a way as to retard [his development]? . . . Leave him in the hands of Him who is the Resurrection! Then prepare self for same. 1786-2

After Susan realized that her desire to communicate with her dead father was interfering with his continuing spiritual development, she was able to let go. She knew without question that she had communicated with him. Afterward, she called upon him only at times when she felt very lonely or in need of his guidance, just as she had sought his guidance in life.

Susan later had a very positive contact with her father after the birth of her granddaughter. Susan was overjoyed at the birth and wished that her father was alive to see Chrissy, the baby. Shortly after Chrissy was born, Susan had a conscious psychic experience of her father being very near to her.

"I felt him communicate with me more than I heard him," Susan said, "but the message was very clear. He said, referring to Chrissy, 'I have known her over here before she came there to you!' He was very happy and was rather amused that I would think he *hadn't* known Chrissy. He was telling me he knew Chrissy from 'the other side.'"[21]

Edgar Cayce frequently said that what is death in the physical realm is a birth to the spiritual worlds, and vice versa. We should take Susan's account of hearing her father as a reassurance that our loved ones continue to be aware of many aspects of our lives, even after their deaths.

A Gift from the Other Side to a Grandchild

When Heather[22] lost her father, Thomas, in May 1992, she was pregnant with her second child, Shirley. After Shirley was born in October 1992, Heather was still deeply grief-stricken; she had wanted so much for her father to live long enough for him to see Shirley. Although time heals all things, Heather continued to find herself beset by grief for years after her father's death. Little Shirley had so many of the characteristics of Heather's father that it was uncanny. This further deepened Heather's sorrow that her father hadn't lived to see this child who was so much like himself. Five years after Thomas's passing, Heather was cleaning her daughter's room when suddenly she heard music that sounded like a music box. She found a stuffed pink rabbit on a shelf that was playing music. Heather couldn't recall having seen the rabbit before. It appeared very old and rather dusty. As she picked it up, she noticed that the rabbit indeed had a music box inside of it.

"I had never seen it before," Heather said, "and I asked Shirley where the rabbit came from. She said, 'My Thomas gave it to me.' I had no idea who she was talking about and then she said, 'You know—your dad—Thomas.' My Dad didn't like to be called 'Grandpa' or 'Grandfather'—he preferred his grandkids to call him Thomas. So I said, 'But Shirley, you never knew Thomas,' and she turned and said, 'Uh-huh! He gave this bunny to me

when I was sleeping. He laid it right next to me.' I didn't
know what to say! Shirley is a very practical, down-to-
earth little girl—hearing those words come out of her
mouth just startled me. I was waiting for her to laugh or
make a joke out of all this, but she was totally serious. I
said, 'Shirley, things like that can't happen.' And she said
again very loud and clear, 'Yes he did! My Thomas came
to me in a dream and talked to me and laid the bunny
down next to me.'"

Heather showed the stuffed rabbit to her relatives,
friends, and acquaintances. None of them had ever seen
it before. Shirley's story has never changed over the
years; she still maintains that her Thomas gave her the
rabbit, and that, yes, she indeed knows her grandfather.
It is interesting to note that the pink rabbit has never
again played music by itself since Heather first discovered it on the shelf in Shirley's room. The materialization was a sign that Heather could now let go of her
grief—death did not separate Thomas from the family.
Her father sent a gift to his granddaughter, and although
it is inexplicable how such a phenomenon occurred, the
manifestation let Heather know without question that
Thomas indeed knows and loves his granddaughter
Shirley.[23]

Edgar Cayce described a similar encounter with his
deceased mother. During a period of great financial difficulty, Edgar Cayce's mother appeared to him and ma-
terialized a silver coin:

> I have had many experiences, and of course, be-
> lieve in materialization, but not for direction, rather
> for assurance. In March 1934 my mother came to
> me and talked with me, even though I was in a New
> Mexico cattle pasture, and materialized a silver dol-
> lar to prove to me I should not worry about money,

but to trust in God and do right and the money for use would come. I took it as assurance, and it has proven so ... 294-161, Reports

A Scientist Researches Apparitions of the Deceased

Years after Dr. Raymond Moody did his groundbreaking research into the near-death experience, he set about to study the phenomenon of visionary encounters with deceased loved ones.

"Many people come back transformed by their near-death experience," Dr. Moody said, "because they see that their loved ones are happy in the afterlife. Having visionary encounters with departed loved ones helps the living in the same way."[24]

Dr. Moody said that professional medical journals have begun exploring after-death communication between the living and the dead in recent years. "There have been articles which have very clearly established that a very high percentage of the population who are bereaved will—within a certain period of time—have an experience of being with the person who has died, and actually communicating with them. In fact, in several medical studies, it was suggested that as many as sixty-six percent of widows have this experience. Widows make up the largest bereaved group. But we also know clinically that bereaved siblings, parents, and children also have these experiences."

Dr. Moody's study into near-death experiences caused a great deal of controversy among his professional medical colleagues in the early 1970s. He came under tremendous fire when he announced that he was going to systematically study after-death communication by facilitating apparitions of the deceased under controlled circumstances. Undaunted, Dr. Moody set about his pioneering research and came up with startling results:

> A number of things came together for me. One
> was simply the recognition that these experiences
> with the deceased are so common. If this is true—
> that it is a common experience—then it stands to
> reason that we would be able to find a way of en-
> hancing the likelihood that somebody could have
> such an experience under controlled circumstances.
> Since [meeting] the deceased [is] a very common
> part of the near-death experience [NDE], it seems
> that if I had some way of bringing about an appari-
> tional encounter under controlled circumstances,
> then I would have an indirect way of studying the
> near-death experience. Seeing departed loved ones
> is tremendously therapeutic. Encountering dead
> relatives is one element of the near-death experi-
> ence that keeps it from being a frightening or trau-
> matic event. Many people come back transformed
> by their NDE *because* they see that their loved ones
> are happy in the afterlife. Having visionary encoun-
> ters with departed loved ones helps the living in the
> same way. It alleviates the fear and the grief. People
> usually are not frightened by seeing apparitions of
> the deceased; they derive a great deal of comfort
> from the experience. This is what prompted me to
> further my research.[25]

Dr. Moody created what he called "The Theater of the
Mind" to do his research, a place where people could
experience visionary encounters with deceased loved
ones. The ancient Greeks had institutions called "psycho-
manteums" where people went to interact with the spirits of the dead. They facilitated the apparitions by using
reflections or mirrors. After researching this ancient tra-

dition, Dr. Moody set about building his own version of a psychomanteum in Anniston, Alabama:

> I found an old grist mill that was built in 1839. It's on a creek in a very rural area in Alabama. I wanted people to be able to do this in a place where it's very memorably pleasant. If this experiment worked, I had a feeling that this was going to be something that might be very, very powerful for these people's emotions. I decorated the place in a way where it would confuse people's sense of time. All of the furniture is antique, and it's put together to make you feel as if you're going back in time.

Dr. Moody created an "apparition chamber," which is a room draped in black velvet. Mounted on the wall—high enough so the person will not see their own reflection—is a very tall Victorian mirror. An easy chair with the legs cut off sits on the floor. The velvet is also mounted on the wall, so the result is that that the person sits in a totally black cocoon, except for the mirrored surface. Behind the person, Dr. Moody places a dim lamp to give a very diffuse light. Because the only illumination in the darkened room comes from behind the person, the light doesn't reflect in the mirror.

"I tell people to simply relax and sit there and wait," Dr. Moody said. "I don't have them worry about time. I go in for them after about an hour and a half. But they're told they can stay in there as long or as little as they wish. After that, they come out and we go through a processing session in which we talk about what happened."[26]

Prior to the participants going into the apparition chamber, Dr. Moody spends a good deal of time interviewing them, discussing their reasons for wanting to see a deceased loved one. In his initial research, he carefully screened the participants and selected those who were professionals, ministers, physicians, nurses, etc., and who didn't have a set core of beliefs about this experience. In other words, he selected those who would be open-minded to *anything* that happened. The results surprised even Dr. Moody. The participants had far more experiences with the deceased than he ever imagined:

> This research really startled me. When I first started setting these ideas out, I made certain assumptions about what my results were going to be. All of those assumptions were absolutely incorrect! I assumed that one out of ten people who go through this would have the experience of seeing a deceased loved one. A reasonable assumption, I thought. I also assumed that if they saw anyone in the mirror, it would be the person whom they chose to see. I also anticipated that the experience would be entirely *visual*, and those who did have an experience would report "seeing a vision." It never entered my mind that there would be any sort of communication between the deceased and the person in the room. I also assumed that the people I had chosen to go through this, if they *did* have an experience, would be very speculative about it.[27]

The amazing facet of this research is that the results were far greater than Dr. Moody ever anticipated. It wasn't one in ten who had a visionary encounter; fifty percent of the twenty-seven people who initially went through the psychomanteum experience had an encounter with a departed loved one.

"Participants didn't necessarily see the person they set out to see," Dr. Moody added. "One man came and we prepared all day for him to see his father. In the evening, it was his deceased business partner who showed up! One woman, a professional counselor, had prepared to see her husband. Instead it was her father she saw."

Another intriguing fact about Dr. Moody's research is that the experiences went far beyond *seeing an apparition*. Participants indeed saw an apparition of their deceased loved one, but they also had conversations with them, and in some cases, the apparitions *moved out from the mirror into the room where the participants were sitting*.

"In many instances," Dr. Moody said, "people had very complex, extended conversations with the person. In many instances, the apparitions of the deceased actually emerged from the mirror and they came into the environment to speak to the person. One person reported that her grandfather actually *hugged* her and wiped away a tear. It was extraordinary!"

Those participants who had an experience with a deceased loved one were profoundly changed by the experience. They *knew* without a doubt that the experience was real, that they had communicated with a loved one who was, for all intents and purposes, no more "dead" than they were. The purpose of Dr. Moody's research was not merely to indulge in manifesting a phenomenon, but to help people allay their grief and sense of loss. Most times when our loved ones and friends die, there is a real sense of "unfinished business." Many of us long to be able to say goodbye, to tell them one more time that we love them. Dr. Moody took painstaking steps to document all of his research for scientific reasons, but the main reason was to help people understand that *there is no death*.

Dr. Moody himself had a profound experience after a session in the psychomanteum. His own grandmother appeared to him, and they had a detailed conversation:

I was prepared to see my maternal grandmother. But the real amazing experience took place later—and that was with my paternal grandmother, who died some years ago. She appeared to me just as real as either of us in this room. We had a long, detailed conversation. I have no doubt in my mind about it. I need to add that those who have experienced this—including myself—report that this isn't some sort of wispy image of a person. The deceased appears just as you and I do—very three-dimensional. I tried to hug my grandmother, and she motioned me back. But otherwise she was completely verbal about everything else. We talked about things that had happened in my childhood that only she knew about. My grandmother even called me by a nickname that only she had used for me. I hadn't even thought of that nickname since I was a child! It was a powerful experience. I'm still processing a lot of what happened in that experience. This is true with most people. Those who have a visionary encounter say it has a profound effect upon their lives. I can attest to that.[28]

Further details of Dr. Moody's pioneering research were published in book form in *Reunions—Visionary Encounters with Departed Loved Ones*. One of the most dramatic cases he documented was the case of a mother who came to Moody so that she might communicate with her son who had battled cancer for several years before he finally died:

The woman missed her son terribly . . . She came to the psychomanteum in hopes of seeing him one more time, just to see if the pain was gone. We prepared all day for the encounter, and then I had her go into the apparition booth. The experience she had was very satisfying. She saw a number of "memory visions," vivid snippets from his childhood. She also reported a strong sense that her son had been present with her in the booth. "He was sitting there with me," she said when she came out. "We sat there together and watched events from our life together."

A few days later I received an incredible call from her. A few days after her visit to my clinic, she awoke from a deep sleep. She didn't simply wake up, she became "hyperawake. Far more awake than normal." There, standing in her room, was her son. As she sat up in bed to look at him, she could see that the ravages of cancer were gone. He now looked vibrant and happy as he had before his disease . . . She stood up and faced her son and began carrying on a conversation . . . They talked about a number of things . . . Finally it dawned on her what was happening. She was talking to an apparition of her son. "I couldn't believe it was him," she said to me. "So I asked if I could touch him." Without a moment's hesitation this apparition of her son stepped forward and hugged her. Then, the woman said, he lifted her right off the ground and over his head.

"What happened was as real as if he had been standing right there," the woman told me. "I now feel as though I can put my son's death behind me and get on fully with my life."[29]

The appearance of the dead, whether in dreams or vision or through the awareness of an unseen but palpable presence, confirms that the complex matrix of interpersonal relationships we cultivate in life continue to grow and evolve in the afterlife just as they do here on earth.

And, according to the Edgar Cayce readings, we can be of help, even after their physical death, to our loved ones who may visit us in dreams, apparitions, or meditation:

> Be sincere with yourself and other outside influences. Even disincarnate entities with and through whom ye may obtain much, will be sincere with you. Sincerity will drive away those that might hinder, but do not use them, do not abuse them. Know that these [entities] come to thee for aid, not to aid you. Aid them! Thus we are admonished to pray for the dead. Pray for the dead, for they only sleep—as the Lord indicated. And if we are able to attune to such, there we may help. Though we may not call back to life as the Son, we can point the way. For there's only one way. And point to that, that is safe in Him, who is the way, the truth and the Light.
> 3657-1

7

Spirit Communication: A Bridge Between Here and Hereafter

I have made no secret of my conviction, not merely that personality persists, but that its continued existence is more entwined with the life of everyday than has been generally imagined; that there is no real breach of continuity between the dead and the living and that methods of intercommunion across what has seemed to be a gulf can be set going in response to the urgent demand of affection . . . as Diotima told Socrates, love bridges the chasm . . .   Sir Oliver J. Lodge

*W*hen Hugh Lynn Cayce began traveling the world and giving lectures on his father's psychic work, some of the most frequently asked questions involved psychic mediumship: Was Edgar Cayce a medium for the spirit world? Did he channel discarnate entities?
Hugh Lynn wrote:

In considering continuity of consciousness after death, the question of greatest interest to many people is the nature of communication between those here and the world beyond the Other Door. It is helpful at this point to understand the source of Edgar Cayce's information. This will answer many of the questions and help enlarge the concept of life after death. Many students of psychical research, and especially those whose personal experiences involve spiritualistic phenomena, assume that the Edgar Cayce phenomenon was of a mediumistic nature. It is not unusual to be asked, "Who was Edgar Cayce's guide or control? A group of doctors must have helped him." Friends inclined to this point of view usually look slightly embarrassed when they hear the readings' own explanation regarding the source of the information. For . . . the explanation *includes* that of communication with entities on other planes of consciousness—but it is *not limited to* such communication as the only source.[1] [author's italics]

In the majority of the readings on record with the Association for Research and Enlightenment, Inc., in Virginia Beach, Virginia, Edgar Cayce's psychic information came from sources that were part of the universal collective consciousness. Most of the information and answers in the readings are worded as if they were being given by a *group*. For example, Cayce would say, "Yes, *we* have the body here," or "Yes, *we* are given the records of the entity," or "Yes, *we* have the conditions of the body before *us*." [author's italics] However, when the psychic connection among Edgar Cayce, the person conducting the reading, and the person for whom the reading was given was in a certain pattern of attunement, a deceased soul (spirit guide) sometimes would provide information and give their identity. This phenomenon was the exception rather than the rule and seemed to occur when individuals and groups *desired* that the information given through Cayce be given by a spirit guide. Whether a psychic is working with automatic writing or trance mediumship or giving readings through the conscious mind, the source of the information that comes through is guided by and reaches the level only of the highest intent and purpose held by both the psychic and the person seeking psychic guidance. Cayce gave a reading that illustrated how such sources operated in his own psychic work and in the work of psychic mediums:

> As has been given, the source [of the readings] may be from the subconscious forces of the body itself, or from the realm of spirit force as may surround the body, or a combination of both, or from a universal consciousness that is the source of life itself . . . the variation dependent upon . . . the attitude of the one seeking, and of that sought . . . In the [physical] body as given, there are channels through which all forces do manifest . . . The lyden [Leydig], or "closed gland" is the keeper—as it were—of the door, that would loose and let either passion or the miracle be loosed to enable those [spirits] seeking to find the Open Door, or the Way to find expression in the . . . sensory forces of a body; whether to fingertips that would write, to eyes that would see, to voice that would speak, to the whole of the system as would feel those impressions that are attuned with those the infinite by their development and association or with those inter-between, or those just passed over, or as to the unseen forces . . . Be satisfied with nothing short of a universal

consciousness, guided or guarded by the Lord of the
Way, or the *way* itself. In *Him* is life! Why be satisfied with a lesser portion than a whole measure?
294-140

There were many helpful unseen forces and spirits
that aided Edgar Cayce in obtaining his psychic information, and sometimes messages were given in the
readings by people who were known to the Cayce family.
On one occasion, a deceased physician gave a message
during a health reading for Hugh Lynn Cayce: "This is
from Dr. Gay," the source said, identifying himself to the
group. Dr. Gay had been closely associated with the
Cayce family many years earlier.

"Edgar and Gertrude Cayce became well acquainted
with . . . Dr. S. Gay while living in Selma, Alabama," Hugh
Lynn wrote. "He operated on Edgar Cayce for appendici-
tis; he delivered [my brother] Edgar Evans . . . in Selma.
Dr. Gay died while the Cayces were still in Selma."[2]

Dr. Gay was a helpful spiritual guide for Hugh Lynn
through the reading, giving medical information and advice just as he had done during his physical life. The
close connection and bond between the Cayces and Dr.
Gay during physical life was not severed by physical
death.

The majority of Cayce's readings were given on medical illness. The treatments he prescribed in the readings
drew from a wide range of medical philosophies. Those
reservoirs of knowledge that Cayce accessed were not
static; they were *unseen worlds* which were inhabited by
the souls of individuals who had studied and practiced
medicine during their time on earth. On rare occasions,
these spirits would identify themselves through the entranced Cayce, as Dr. Gay had done. In a reading for
Edgar Cayce's seventy-five-year-old father, L.B., a Dr. Hill

(L.B.'s physician who had long been deceased at the time of the reading), "tuned in" to give L.B. the same helpful advice he had given during his physical life. Hill had been the elder Cayce's physician for many years, and their close association enabled him to give a final word of medical advice at the close of the reading:

> Do not get the feet wet—[except] to bathe them—of course bathe them—but don't get them wet outside. Do not get the head damp. Do not remain where drafts or cold will produce quick congestion, especially while these changes are taking place. Many years will be added to this life *through* the *adhering* to these suggestions. This is Hill. We are through with this reading. 304-16

Edgar Cayce's secretary made the following notation at the bottom of the reading:

> When Edgar Cayce awoke from [this] reading, Mrs. Cayce told him that "old Dr. Hill" had come through. It seems that he was a medical doctor they had known in Kentucky when they were young; he had also at one time been the family doctor for Mr. L.B. Cayce. He was also known by Dr. Thomas B. House, who was in the room at the time of the reading.

Instances such as these of spirit communication in the readings illustrate the continuity of life beyond physical death. Dr. Hill and Dr. Gay hadn't changed their interests after physical death; they had only *changed environments*. An individual's capacity to be a source of healing, guidance, and counsel for others is not a *human* quality; it is a *spiritual* quality. The compassion to want

to help others heal—emotionally, physically, or spiritually—is a faculty of the soul and spirit and is not buried
with the body at physical death. Regardless of whether
the soul is in physical form or has passed on, it always
has the ability to guide and to give comfort and assistance to others. The soul of Dr. Gay not only was willing
to help give the Cayce family medical advice from the
afterlife, but in a subsequent reading, he offered his ser-
vices to be "on hand" to assist Gertrude Cayce in her
work conducting the readings. Dr. Gay interrupted the
posthypnotic suggestion to bring Cayce out of the reading. He asked Gertrude to wait a moment·because he
wanted to offer his insights on how Cayce's psychic
work operated and to give advice on how best to carry it
out:

> Here, Sister—before you change this, let me give
> you a little piece of advice concerning what you are
> working with . . . [this information] will possibly aid
> you in understanding just what takes place, and as
> to how you—personally may assist or may aid the
> individual seeking to know that as may be helpful,
> beneficial to themselves or their loved ones [through
> the readings] . . . This is the condition that is ever
> present when such information is obtained: When
> the consciousness is laid aside, there is that which
> takes place much in the same manner as the spring
> to an automatic curtain roller [window shade]. This,
> then, is able to be pulled down or raised up with the
> release of the spring. *Some* call this spiritual, or
> spirit, communication. Some call it the ability to
> gain the force of the activities of the fourth dimen-
> sion—which is *nearer* correct than any explanation
> that may be given. For it [the fourth dimension] . . .
> that is of the inter-between, or that of the border-

land—which all individuals occupy through that period of gaining consciousness of that sphere they themselves occupy . . . Now each individual seeks experiences, see? Each individual must experience conditions to become aware of that being present or existent in their *own* experience . . . Then, know, whenever there is the wholehearted desire of all seeking such, there may be the perfect action of the roller or spring, or there may be the perfect application of the information that may be gained. But Sister, know this—whenever you, yourself, are in the position of the questionnaire, or the one seeking to gain for another such information [through the readings], call *me*—I will answer. This is Gay. We are through. 538-28

When Dr. Gay was alive, numerous people acted as a conductor of Cayce's psychic readings, and at times Gay questioned the scruples and sincerity of the conductors. Prior to Gertrude Cayce acting as conductor for the majority of the readings, some people that Dr. Gay knew seized the opportunity to ask the sleeping Cayce questions that were of a decidedly materialistic nature, such as "Which horse should I bet on at the track?" A later reading said that using Cayce's abilities to obtain such trivial information was like using a delicate surgical knife to do nothing more than sharpen pencils! When the conductor of Cayce's reading made such a diversion, the effect upon the waking Cayce was devastating: He would wake up with a blinding headache and feel very ill. Further devastating was the knowledge that the conductor of Cayce's readings couldn't be trusted to stay close to the spiritual ideals of his psychic gift.

In his message, Dr. Gay offered to help when and where needed. Because of his compassionate spirit, Dr.

Gay was offering to be a spirit guide during the readings, to help Cayce stay on track and attune to the very highest sources of healing information. Again, we have another example that the best of our spiritual selves, our virtues, goes with the soul after physical death. While the readings themselves acknowledged that many unseen presences were aiding Cayce in his psychic work, they cautioned against looking to any spirit guide to be the sole director of the information that came through Edgar Cayce. The readings said that if the group surrounding Cayce looked for a specific guide or control to direct the psychic information, they would be putting a limit on the spiritual sources of information available to them. The most sincere spirit guides act very much like Frances Banks did for Helen Greaves, during her dictation of *Testimony of Light*. Frances did not acknowledge herself as the Source of all wisdom and knowledge, she said she merely was a guide, passing along what she had learned so far in her after-death journey, without making her individual self the focus of the communications. Cayce's readings indicate this should be the criterion for delving into the areas of mediumship and channeling. A constructive spirit guide will direct the individual to seek ever higher levels of spiritual knowledge and wisdom, information that helps them come closer to the Creator. Spirit entities who claim to be *the source* of the spiritual information coming through the channel, rather than a guide or aid, are usually spirits from a less-evolved and more earthbound dimension of consciousness.

In 1935, a reading was given by Edgar Cayce that illustrated workings of the unseen forces, and emphasized the importance of the group's attunement to the very Source of life itself, rather than reliance upon a specific spirit guide to direct Cayce's psychic work. The sources that expressed themselves in the reading are quite impressive; yet, at times they grew impatient because the questions were centered around finding out the identities of the spirit guides who were aiding Edgar Cayce:

> We—from the source of all knowledge that is promised in Him—salute thee, and give that which will be helpful to those who seek to be in the ministry of those influences and forces that make for more and more awareness of the divine in each and every soul ... Then, from the heights of those experiences, those hierarchies in the earth and in the air, we come as messengers of truth to those who will hear, and question.
>
> (Q) For the better or more rational presentation of the work of Edgar Cayce to the world, will you, if you consider same in order, kindly inform us of Thine Identity and the source or sources from which you bring us the information given in answer to our questions in the readings ...
>
> (A) From the universal forces that are acceptable and accessible to those who in earnestness *open* their minds, their souls, to the wonderful words of truth and light.
>
> (Q) To what extent are the Masters ... directing the activities of Edgar Cayce? Who are the Masters directly in charge?
>
> (A) Messengers from the higher forces that may manifest from the Throne of grace itself ... Those that are directed by the Lord of lords, the King of kings, Him that came that ye might be one with the Father.
>
> (Q) Is Saint Germain among them? ...
>
> (A) These are all but messengers of the Most High ...

(Q) Is Saint Germain among them?
(A) When needed.
(Q) Please give us Thine Identity.
(A) He that seeks that has not gained the control
·seeks damnation to his own soul! Control thine inner self that *ye* may *know* the true life and light! For
he that would name the Name must have become
perfect in himself!
(Q) If Mr. Cayce is a member and a messenger of
the Great White Brotherhood, how do the Masters
wish him to proceed and should not his activities
henceforth be presented as Their Work?
(A) As the work of the *Master* of masters, that may
be presented when in those lines, those accords
necessary through the White Brotherhood. This—
this—*this*, my friends, even but *limits*; while in Him
is the Whole. Would thou make of thyself, of thyselves,
a limited means of activity? . . . Let *Him* that is the
author, that is the finisher, that *is* the Life . . . let *Him*
alone be thy guide! Dost He call any soul into service, *then* by name will He—does He—designate . . .
254-83

The reading strongly encouraged Cayce's group to
look to the Creator as the source of the information and
said that, should a spirit entity come through the readings to give a message, that spirit should be treated as a
benevolent messenger sent by the Source. If the group
relied upon or looked to a singular discarnate spirit to
guide the psychic information, then Cayce would not be
able to access any information *higher* than the entity directing.

The following reading gives a detailed explanation on
the advantages of relying upon the Universal Force to be
the guide and the disadvantages of the sole reliance

upon specific spirit entities as the sources of psychic information:

> To call upon the Infinite is much greater, much more satisfying, much more worth while in the experience of an individual soul than being guided or directed merely by an entity outside of self that—*as* self—*is* being in a state of transition *or* development. There may be experiences when individual entities may proclaim or indicate their own activity by a name, but . . . a name immediately sets metes and bounds about the abilities . . . Not that (as a very crude example) one would send for a plumber to judge a painting. One would not seek a well-digger to judge a musical interpretation. One would not seek for those merely because they had experienced a view without the development or training. But, as God's purpose is to *glorify* the individual man (or soul) in the earth, so the highest purpose of an individual soul or entity is to glorify the Creative Energy or God in the earth. Should the Maker use a gnome, a fairy, an angel, a developing entity *for* a guide, alright—for a specific direction; for He hath given His angels charge concerning thee, and *thy* god, thy face, is ever before the Throne of the Infinite. 338-3

It is easy to become distracted by the phenomenon of after-death communication, particularly when a bereaved person has a visionary or dream encounter with a deceased loved one. The bereaved can become so caught up in the *phenomenon* of the apparition of the deceased that they miss the message the loved one has come to deliver. Hugh Lynn Cayce once said that if, in meditation, we encounter a deceased loved one, a spirit

guide, the Buddha, or even Jesus, we should acknowledge with reverence their presence, take their message
to heart, and go back to meditating. They are called
"guides" for a very good reason: The spirits of those who
come to us or give messages through psychic readings
or appear in dreams are *guiding influences that come to
help us increase our awareness of our unity and closeness
with the Creator.* Our deceased loved ones, according to
the Cayce readings, can offer positive guidance in our
journey through the earth and help direct us toward
greater spiritual unfoldment.

One of the earliest recorded readings in the Cayce collection was given for a thirty-eight-year-old man who
was told that his mother was acting as his spirit guide.
From the other side, she was attempting to influence
him in a more constructive direction in his life. At the
time of the reading, the man was in a state of inner and
outer turmoil and was being dragged down and away
from a spiritually centered life through "environmental
associations," as Cayce put it. From the unseen realms,
the man's deceased mother was attempting to guide him
in a better direction:

> In this man's body we find that he has in his ac-
> tions, and treatment of life to himself and those as-
> sociated with him, is governed by his environments
> from day to day, or the class of people he associates
> with more than by teachings of his mother who is
> the guide. We all have a guide, either dead or living.
> Some are guided by dead, and some by living spir-
> its. This man's guide is his mother. There is a war-
> ring of spirits mental and metaphysically . . . Now
> this association has brought within his own mind
> those things that he knows are contrary to his guide,
> or his mother, as it happens to be in this case, so it

causes him in his own mind to treat his associates
not with proper respect also to his mother . . . To
better the condition . . . apply those things to keep
him under the rule or under the supervision of the
guide [his mother] more than his associates . . . Appeal through the sensory system [meditation,
prayer, etc.], to his better [higher] self. All guides
whether spiritual or material, have the power to influence their subjects. 4348-1

Many people can look back at their lives and recall the
sense or awareness that a deceased love one was near
them during one of life's crossroads such as a time of crises or when a major decision had to be made. At such
times, we are in the presence of guardian influences
even though we might feel very alone. Cayce said that if
the man in reading 4348-1 were to "appeal to his better
self," then he would experience greater peace and less
turmoil. If the man were to take time each day in prayer
and meditation to ask for divine help and aid in devel-
oping a more spiritually-centered life, then he would be
putting himself under the positive influence of his
guardian spirit, his mother. His mother would then become a channel through which divine aid could come
into his life and his world. The man might identify with
the spirit of his mother, but in the cosmic sense, the help
would come from the Creator, who *sent* his mother to
help guide him.

When people become more psychically sensitive and
spiritually aware, they also become closer to a dimension of consciousness in the after-death realms where
many souls are seeking expression in the material
world—some for good purposes and some for bad. The
soul's ultimate destiny, according to the Cayce readings,
is to reenter into a state of conscious communion and

oneness with the Creator. When we develop psychic awareness and sensitivity, it is of utmost importance not to lose sight of that premise. If that ideal is lost, a person can become caught up in the *spirit entities themselves* and, thus, be overwhelmed and possibly possessed by less-developed or earthbound spirits masquerading as teachers or avatars. The readings said the criteria for delving into these areas, particularly mediumship, are to always say a prayer of protection prior to entering into an altered state of consciousness or deep meditation, and to ask that the guides who may be encountered be sent only from the Christ Consciousness or from the universal realms of love and light. Holding that in mind, a person will not get "lost" or distracted by any negative spirit entities.

There have been many gifted and famous psychic mediums throughout history who didn't lose sight of this precept. They used their mediumistic abilities to provide assistance and aid from the Divine to those who were seeking help and healing. One psychically sensitive woman from Virginia who became an adept said that whenever she encountered a discarnate spirit, she would ask them, "Do you come in the name of Christ?" She noticed that those who were of the more earth-earthy consciousness tended to disappear, and the ones who were of a higher spiritual light would remain and guide her through the reading. The spirit guides who were most helpful to her were the ones who responded, "Yes, I come in the name of the Most High and in the name of Love." At that point, the woman would grant them permission to provide information to the person or persons in the room who were seeking spiritual guidance. For the better part of the thirty years that the woman has been a practicing intuitive, she has never had a negative encounter, nor has her spiritual work been hindered or interfered with by earthbound or mischievous spirits.

Jane Roberts, one of the world's most well-documented mediums, never encountered a negative experience during the two decades that she channeled a spirit entity named Seth. In late 1963, Roberts spontaneously lapsed into an altered state of consciousness while writing poetry in her studio in Elmira, New York. Roberts had no background in psychic phenomena prior to this experience. But in that moment, Roberts felt as she were suddenly propelled into an expansive state of awareness far removed from her physical environment. Her husband, artist Robert Butts, came into the studio just as she was coming back to waking consciousness, and she described her unusual experience:

> Suddenly my consciousness left my body, and my mind was barraged by ideas that were astonishing and new to me at the time. On return to my body, I discovered that my hands had produced an automatic script . . . The notes were even titled— *The Physical Universe as Idea Construction.* Because of that experience, I began doing research into psychic activity . . . [3]

Her research led her and her husband to experiment with a Ouija board, which they borrowed from a neighbor. "After the first few sessions," Roberts wrote, "the pointer spelled out messages that claimed to come from a personality called Seth. Neither Rob nor I had any psychic background, and when I began to anticipate the board's replies, I took it for granted that they were coming from my subconscious. Not long after, however, I felt impelled to say the words aloud, and within a month I was speaking for Seth while in a trance state . . . "[4]

Roberts proceeded slowly, and she and her husband decided to see where this strange journey was headed. Little did they know that their pioneering exploration would result in more than twenty published books and essays. A number of the books were dictated solely by Seth himself, who described himself as "a personality essence no longer focused in physical reality."

Roberts and Butts approached the Seth material with healthy skepticism, discernment, and very open minds. "We were explorers," Roberts said, "and we were going to be careful about exploring something we didn't understand. But we were going to do it."[5]

They carefully documented every step of their journey, Roberts's husband acting as stenographer during the twice-weekly "Seth sessions," taking down Seth's dissertations in shorthand and then typing and indexing them. Unlike Edgar Cayce, Roberts didn't need a preparation period to lie down and "go to sleep." She was fully conscious right up to the point where Seth began speaking.

"In the beginning I paced the floor constantly in trance," Roberts wrote. "I refused to sit down because I had read about Cayce . . . he lay down on the couch. And I thought, 'No, not for me! I'm not going to lie down!' Because I figured if I didn't like what was going to happen I could run. It was *several years* before I allowed myself to sit down!"[6]

Seth had a definite presence and personality and a jovial demeanor. His personality was totally unlike Roberts's. When Seth spoke through her, Roberts's facial features changed dramatically, appearing distinctly masculine. Her soft, lilting voice, with a pronounced New England accent, also changed. Seth spoke in a deep baritone with a slight European accent. The only film footage of a recorded Seth session shows that the transformation from Jane Roberts to Seth is complete and astonishing. During the twice-weekly, two-hour sessions that were held in Roberts's home, Seth took breaks, and Roberts easily slipped out of trance. Like Edgar Cayce, Roberts came out of trance to ask questions about the material. She had no conscious recall during trance states.

Seth gave voluminous material on the nature of the soul, and the continuity of life beyond physical death. Seth's information parallels that in the Cayce readings that said the soul passes to a dimension of its own making after death:

> There is not just one dimension in which non-physical consciousness resides, any more than there is only one country on your planet or planets within your solar system. My environment now, is not the one in which you will find yourself immediately after death. I cannot help speaking humorously, but you must die many times before you enter this particular plane of existence. Birth is much more of a shock than death. Sometimes when you die you do not realize it, but birth almost always implies a sharp and sudden recognition. So there is no need to fear death. And I, who have died more times than I care to tell, write this . . . to tell you so . . . You must understand that no objective reality exists but that which is created by consciousness. Consciousness always creates form, and not the other way around. So my environment is a reality of existence created by myself and others like me, and it represents the manifestation of our development.[7]

> My field is education, and my particular interest is that these [seemingly paranormal] abilities be understood and investigated, for they are not un-

natural, but inherent . . . I am indeed aware of the difficulties which shall be encountered. I have said this often—I am no misty-eyed ghostly spirit, materializing in the middle of the night. I am simply an intelligent personality no longer bound by your physical laws . . . [8]

In the early period of their work, Jane Roberts and her husband wondered if Seth was a deeper part of her own subconscious mind. Although all souls are connected at the subconscious level, Seth was indeed a separate identity. His *modus operandi*, however, was the *avenue of Jane Roberts's subconscious mind*. This was the avenue that also enabled Edgar Cayce to diagnose illness in people in other states and countries. He traveled through the dimensions of humanity's collective unconscious. This is the avenue, too, through which we receive messages from the deceased. The subconscious is a bridge among the worlds, and everyone (whether conscious of it or not) receives guidance from spirit guides, angels, and what Cayce called the "unseen forces."

"I am not Roberts's subconscious," Seth once said, "though I speak *through* it. It is the atmosphere through which I can come to you, as the air is the atmosphere through which the bird flies."[9]

In one session, Seth described his perspectives on the nature of life and self-unfoldment:

There are journeys of consciousness that no one can take except you. And yet as you take them, you take steps, in other terms, for others. You leave marks for your brothers and sisters to follow in their own explorations; cards that say, "I have been here, the place is safe, I leave you a sign of peace." Your *being* alone is important, and has a validity beyond any philosophy. That is the message that you are trying to give to yourself. You are trying to rediscover for yourself after centuries in your terms, centuries of myths and distortions, the validity of your own being. I ask you not to trust the validity of *my* being, which is none of your concern. Trust the validity of *your* being—which is very much of your concern . . . [10]

Jane Roberts's explorations and experiments with the psychic took her down many avenues and through many doorways prior to her own death in 1984. As Seth said above, the journeys of our fellows are *our journeys*. The more we learn about such inner explorations of the worlds of the soul, the more accustomed we become to ourselves as entities that existed long before and, most importantly, continue that existence after physical death. The life and living, as Cayce said repeatedly, is continuous.

By the mid 1970s, Jane Roberts and her husband had recorded a large collection of published and unpublished works. Jane continued her trance sessions in which Seth gave regular dictation. Seth dictated several books, including *Seth Speaks—The Eternal Validity of the Soul* and *The Nature of Personal Reality*. Through Jane Roberts, Seth meticulously delved into the nature of consciousness and higher dimensional realities. He provided each book title, table of contents, and chapter heading, and every word of text in his own books. Seth was adept not only as a teacher, but also as a writer and editor. The editors at Prentice-Hall Press were astonished by Seth's abilities because Seth provided a first— and final—draft of each book.

Like Edgar Cayce, Jane Roberts didn't know exactly where the Seth material was leading, but she and her husband were, first and foremost, spiritual pioneers.

They were endlessly surprised by the number of subjects that Seth introduced. They were further astonished when Jane was introduced to the idea of transcribing an "after-death journal" of the renowned philosopher, psychologist, and the pioneering psychic investigator, William James:

> In November, 1974, I first became "acquainted" with William James, the well-known American psychologist . . . who died in 1910. Mentally I saw a small paperback book, opened midway through, and I knew that it was titled *The Varieties of Religious States.* At first the book was in miniature, but it grew larger, so that I could read it clearly, sentence by sentence. At the same time I knew that somehow the book was written by William James . . . I explained to Rob what was happening. Then, while he took notes, I read out loud the pages I saw. We both took it for granted that the image of the book in my mind's eye was symbolic.[11]

The image, however, was not symbolic. Just as the birth of the Seth material came in a spontaneous image while Roberts was writing, yet another birth was taking place: According to Seth, the consciousness of William James had "networked" with Roberts. It is rather amusing to note that Roberts wasn't drawn to the idea of exploring James's material—from his most recent and famous earth life—or the life he now led in the realms unseen. But as spiritual investigators, Roberts and James were very similar. Roberts's universal questions about the nature of reality, life after death, the soul, etc., went out from her like a radio signal. Because of her psychic sensitivity, she was able to tune in to the spirit of James, who had, during his lifetime, asked the same questions with equal passion. Seth gave his own views about the coming together of William James and Jane Roberts:

> There are often great challenges to which you respond. You pick these for your own reasons. In doing so, you often change affiliations. In conventional terms . . . through Ruburt [Roberts], certain challenges and purposes left unsatisfied by James have been picked up by Rubert; and to that extent a portion of William James's consciousness is merged with Ruburts's . . . Your drives, desires, plans, and purposes while uniquely yours, also in their way belong to the species as a whole . . . They are handed down, so to speak, to those who are attuned to them. You pass them on. James, *to some extent, now*, sees his unanswered questions sifted through the other unique consciousness [Roberts], so that they are given a different slant . . . James's consciousness is to some extent, then, reflected through Ruburts's, shining with a different cast, and henceforth forming a new combination—one that is original and represents a new creative world view . . . [12]

Roberts continued conducting the regular Seth sessions, and two years later, James came "knocking" on the door of her psyche, ready to dictate his views. One morning, Roberts and Butts were eating breakfast and, suddenly, the entire first paragraph of *The Afterdeath Journal of an American Philosopher* filled Roberts's mind. She quickly went to her typewriter and began typing what would be the first and final draft of James's after-death journal. The process was a cooperative experience between Roberts and James; their two universes came together and, out of that unity, James again found expression in the material world.

Edgar Cayce's readings indicated that perfect communication between the other side and those in the earth relies upon the willingness of both sides to communicate. Once Roberts felt comfortable with the idea of transcribing James's views, the doorway or bridge between the worlds became accessible.

"The delivery of the manuscript developed its own set of conventions along the way," Roberts wrote. "Most of it was written automatically, first and final draft directly on the typewriter. Much of it came in a surprising way, though, when I was sketching and thought I was finished with the day's writing. As a result, my small sketchpads were filled with page upon page of scribbled James material that I took down with whatever colored pen I happened to be using at the moment. Then I'd have to type up that material the following day, and often while I was doing *that*, James would begin again with new material."[13]

During dictation, Roberts had impressions of the historic James walking up and down the living room, arms folded, deep in thought. She became intimately familiar with and grew quite fond of James—his historic self and his personal self. It's been said that James's search for evidence of life beyond death was at times all-consuming. His commentaries through Roberts indicated he had found great relief in the continuity of his life on the other side. In the early sessions, James described his reasons for coming into the world to dictate his views:

. . . as one who dabbled in psychology and religion both, and attempted to form from each one unified philosophy, I feel in some regard responsible for those insights I might have added to such issues—yet did not. I find myself determined to lend what Light I can upon such matters, particu-

larly since my experience of time is now so luxuri-
ous . . . [14]

In the world in which once I so gladly took my
place, the dead have few rights for their existence
goes unrecognized, and no psychologist prepares
them for the transitions that occur as the soul
moves into realms for which no earthly education
can prepare it. Being of melancholy mind, I anticipated my own death so often, however, and built
such dire forebodings of dissolution and decay that
the fact of death came as an intellectual and emotional revelation of unspeakable degree, whose
brightness dimmed all other events of my life, so
that by contrast my death became the crowning
achievement of my life. This need not have been the
case, however, for had I understood and followed
the natural contours of the mind, then I would have
allowed the unconventional aspects of my heart
and mind alike greater freedom . . . My world was a
lively one that saw the birth of psychology, not realizing that it was swaddled in the placenta of old religious beliefs and still immersed in ancient prejudices
. . . I was at once [during physical life] overly credu-
lous and overly critical, so that my emotions and
intellect rarely met as friends on any common
ground, but rather as adversaries geared for battle
. . . Freed by death from the conventional frame-
works of thought and belief that surrounded me, I
have gained in death insights and comprehensions
of the greatest consequence . . . [15]

The manuscript of James's postmortem writings
through Roberts were studied by James Windsor, Ph.D.,
a longtime student and professor of James's teachings. "I

am absolutely convinced of the authenticity of the writings," Windsor said. "James delved into religious mysticism and spiritualism for as much of his own musings as well as professional study. It would certainly be like the professor to give his 'views from there' after death. The writings [through Roberts] should be studied and applied side-by-side with James's earlier work in *Varieties of Religious Experience*. These spirit writings complete, in my opinion, the early writings of James."[16]

William James's existence at the time of his work with Jane Roberts wasn't far removed from the physical world. It seems that James was residing in the astral realms, where he was still very much the person who existed in the nineteenth century. He was aware of the earth and his former life, but his perceptions of both had changed. He said that when he focused his attention on the physical world, he saw it like the "negative of a photograph." He still pursued his activities and interests related to the study of varied dimensions of consciousness, but in a much more expansive way. Once he was no longer hindered by three-dimensional reality, he was able to *experience* the concepts he so diligently studied while on earth. From his after-death vantage point, James was able to describe the world and the life he had known. He saw the intricate details of how each thought is indeed a thing and, as Edgar Cayce said, that thoughts impact us and the universe at large, long after our physical deaths:

> In your terms, after physical death the division between living and non-living has little meaning . . . There are gradations of consciousness, rather; divisions, with one blending into another . . . It is difficult for me to say how my experience of time has altered. I can "see" the world's thought patterns as I described them and the world's emotional

forms "at once," as you might see the clouds if you were high enough above the earth. I can also "see" my own life in the same way, in its entirety as I knew it, but also in ways that were unfamiliar to me then. The events of my own life appear open-ended to me; I see what I did, but also what I might have done, and can perceive the energy I sent out in directions that I did not take consciously. I can track my own influence then, see the thousands—no, millions—of people I affected, as each of you affects the earth and its populace in far greater terms than you realize. Each contact, direct or not, counts and ripples outwards so that each person's life sends out lines of contact intersecting with others on a psychic level . . . So after death, watching the tracks of one's own influence is perhaps the most fascinating of endeavors . . . Most interesting of all, perhaps, these lifelines begin before birth and continue after it. The traces of my own life still intersect with and affect those living . . . [17]

The thoughts we think, the prayers we offer, the good we do in this world live on, influencing and affecting not only our souls after death, but also the world we leave behind. In other words, nothing ever dies.

William James, speaking through Roberts, also discussed how the dead view their relationships with the living. He said that the deceased are still very much aware of their loved ones on earth, but he said they do not "miss" them the way people on earth do after someone dies. The deceased have entered a new world of experiences and higher learning, and, just as we might get caught up in our own pursuits after taking a new job or moving to a new city, they easily get caught up and absorbed in new activities and worlds after death:

They [the dead] do not feel absent from the living, only present in an entirely different fashion
than the living can fathom. The dead in their way
are jealous of their freedom, and sometimes their
communications take the form of hasty, "Yes, I'm
all right" messages, shouted over a mental shoul-
der. Some people forget to send letters when they
travel, caught up as they are in new experiences.
Similarly, the dead are so involved in their own adventures that sometimes they ignore the nagging of
the living, whose thoughts rise up like mental kites
with reminders, saying, "Why haven't you written?"[18]

Edgar Cayce gave a reading that parallels James's post-
mortem views:

In the various forms of communication, why, *why*,
is such communication so often of seemingly an
unnecessary nature, or seemingly inadequate to the
mind of the soul entity, as understood by the mind
of one hearing, seeing, or experiencing, such a
communication? As may be illustrated: ... The message as may be received from the boy just passed
into the spirit world, and able through mediumistic
forces of someone to communicate to mother, "All
is well. Do not grieve. Do not long for the change."
Such seems to be in the nature of rebuke to a conscious mind when momentous questions as might
be propounded, could be, or would be ... given ...
Those in the astral plane are not always ready [to
communicate with the living]. Those in the physical plane are not always ready ... 5756-4

Cayce went on to say that the deceased still have their

moods and their individual attitudes as they had during their earthly life. There are periods where those on the other side aren't in the mood to talk! For many people who anxiously await a message to come through their dreams or meditation from a deceased friend or relative, Cayce's readings indicate that the dead are very busy indeed, particularly during the early stages after physical death. On some occasions, however, souls that have developed the spiritual consciousness to be aware after physical death will communicate with the living in the early weeks or months after physical death.

Dorothy Rohrbach,[19] an intuitive and healer from Michigan, began getting impressions of Carleton Ryding, a close friend who had recently died. Dorothy became aware of Carleton's presence while conducting a therapeutic healing session on her friend, Margarete Kammer. Carleton had been a very spiritually-minded man during his lifetime, and he had a close association with both Dorothy and Margarete. The relationship among the three made communication with Carleton much easier. Not only did Dorothy pick up messages from Carleton, but other members of his spiritual study group and family members began hearing from him. The chronicle of his journey seemed to be of utmost importance to him, based on the barrage of messages people were receiving.

"Carleton was a very spiritual soul who lived with inner guidance and had many psychic experiences," Margarete said. "Within two weeks of his passing (June 6, 1996), his friends and some family started to hear from him—in dreams, voice, touch and automatic writing."

Carleton was tremendously active during his sixty-eight years of life, and he was vitally interested in spirituality and psychical research. He was actively involved with a *Search for God* spiritual study group, for more than twenty years. He had long discussions with his friends about the nature of the soul and the afterlife. Consequently, when he began "showing up" through the dreams and psychic experiences of his friends, none of his close circle were surprised.

"Carleton was always studying," Margarete said. "Everything from angels to life after death, to spiritual healing." She understood that the information that came through Dorothy and their group was Carleton's way of continuing with his work and studies, just as he had diligently pursued them during his physical life.

"His friends were pleased to hear from him," Margarete said. "Although we will miss him, we no longer grieve for him."

Margarete inquired during a healing session with Dorothy how Carleton was faring in the non-physical world. On January 29, 1998, Carleton gave a simple but profound overview of the continuity of life and the lessons we come to earth to learn. The following is a condensed transcript of Dorothy's reading.

"Carleton wants to say something," Dorothy began. "He is aware of the time you are in communication with him. He is not always able to communicate every time you think of him. It's similar to voice mail. Even if you only 'think' the message, it is stored somewhere and he gets it. He may not respond because of what he is doing elsewhere. But he is getting every single message, loudly and clearly."

Margarete was able to ask questions during the reading session:

(Q) Is Carleton able to tell me anything about the other side?
(A) Yes. He has gone through two more levels since you were here for your last healing session.

He doesn't know what you would understand about the other side. There is a progression of places of energy levels. Scripture calls it "mansions." Not necessarily meaning they are all magnificent but there are various places to live which are much better than Earth. There is a level to go to when a soul crosses first cross over. Not all souls get to that first level immediately after death. Carleton did, because he was [spiritually] aware, wanted to, and was ready. Souls who commit suicide or don't believe in an afterlife can hover. Some haven't finished their business, and think they are still living [on earth]. There is a level where souls are debriefed, meet guides, meet other souls they know. A soul has a chance to stay there and they can create whatever it is that they physically miss on Earth, if they want to. And they can stay there as long as they want to. At some point the soul comes to an awareness that there has to be more. It is not quite heaven. When they reach that conclusion, they are ready to move on. At these various levels there are always tutors available. The layers/levels we are talking about are not always successive layers. So not everybody starts at "A" and goes to "B" and "C." [There are] different systems. So the levels are almost as unique as the souls. At any level there are options to get help. And the help can be to help settle something below you; something that wasn't finalized at some lower level or on Earth. The help can be to better acclimate to where the soul is. The help can be to determine where the next step is.

(Q) When would a soul decide to return to Earth?

(A) It is different for each individual soul. At one point, the soul begins to sense . . . or would have an awareness of "I think I need to go back now. " There is a type of nudge. [The soul then] goes to some clearing center, similar to [Emigration] Headquarters and at that spot, there is an overview of the future life with a supportive group of beings. For example, if one comes back to earth with a certain soul as the mother, this soul as the father, living over in this area with this color skin, facing these social circumstances, this is likely what will happen, etc. So the soul gets a chance to see . . . not every moment of every day, but the highlights, the major things that the soul will experience. The future spiritual support team for the soul (guides) give their input in this preview. They may be able to say, "In this hard spot, if you get on a spiritual path, we'll be more able to assist your ability to respond. You may become aware of additional options." In a sense, the soul signs a contract of the upcoming life issues after the preview. Some souls come in with several different paths that they might be able to take, depending on certain key junctures. Other souls come in with "That's the way, it's going to be; there are no other choices." It's not done with the sense of God's punishing or judging. It's done with the sense of the soul being the primary priority and what is best to help free the soul of the energetic debris that it left behind on earth. The soul will come in when it is appropriate astrologically and vibratorially for the soul and the family. This brief overview and explanation is very elementary but creates a beginning framework of understanding.

When we leave the earth, it resembles leaving a house. And while we were living in that house, we had all these various rooms. The spiritually attuned people are more aware of more of their rooms and tend to pay attention to them. This is a broad generalization, again, but it will help to put some understanding into place. [The spiritually attuned souls] tend to spend more time in their rooms, and keep them in better condition. They use more of what is there. Any relationship, any emotion, any unfinished anything of an agenda that the soul does not free and release through love, grace, and forgiveness remains in that house. So when the soul leaves for the last time [at death] from that body and goes to the other side, anything left from that one lifetime resides right within that home. No one else has permission or the capability to come in and clean up after the mess the soul left. The soul has to do it, itself. So it has to come back on earth and it has to pick up the debris or some of it that it left it behind. The less spiritually aware they have been, the more emotionally volatile and self-righteous, etc., the more debris there is. One powerful spiritual lifetime can wipe out a lot of debris. In real terms, on Earth, we would say "I'm going to call up a house cleaning service and I'm going to have a crew clean this house in a week." In spiritual terms, that would be equivalent to saying . . . that you are going to forgive everybody, you are going to give grace; you are going to love . . . That erases it [the debris]. There is so much potency to a spiritual path of grace, forgiveness, and love.[20]

It isn't by chance then that each soul is in its current life experience. "All the world's a stage," Shakespeare said, and we are not only the actors, but we are writing the script, directing, producing, and creating our storylines and plot. The earth is a dimension where, according to Cayce, all of the Universal Forces may be applied in three dimensions. Life is an unseen essence that flows

through us and *through* the material world; it does not
have its source in physical terms. The lessons or chal-
lenges each soul faces during its lifetime are opportunities to manifest its spiritual expression in a material
world. When the soul departs the material world's stage,
it moves into a dimension where it can review the life
just lived—every thought, every deed, every event—and
the life is measured by how much love the soul imprinted
upon the world of three dimensions. All along the way,
we can be reassured that we do not travel this road alone.
We are, and will eventually become aware that we are, in
the loving companionship of many guides, spirits, and
other messengers sent by the Creator.

"Love is the glue that holds the world together,"
George Ritchie once said. "God is busy building a race of
[people] who know how to love. I believe that the fate of
the earth itself depends on the progress we make . . . As
for what we'll find in the next world, here too I believe
that what we'll discover there depends on how well we
get on with the business of loving, here and now."[21]

8

The Shadowlands:
Earthbound Souls and Hell

"As the tree falls . . . so does it lie" . . . For the beginnings in the
next experiences [after death] are ever tempered by . . . the
purpose . . . of the entity in the experience before.

                                        Edgar Cayce Reading 5260-1

On a winter day in 1935, Edgar Cayce had one of the
most terrifying psychic experiences of his life; it
was a day on which he would come to new and startling
realizations about the psychic world and the darker dimensions beyond death.

A forty-year-old woman, Marlene Miller[1], had come to
the Cayce household in Virginia Beach, Va., for a psychic
reading. She had heard that Cayce could answer questions about the purpose and spiritual mysteries of life.
Edgar Cayce's longtime secretary, Gladys Davis, had cor-

responded with Marlene for a time prior to her arrival for the reading. As was usual in the everyday routine of his psychic work, Cayce rarely knew who was scheduled for a reading until his secretary told him just before the session—unless they came to visit prior to the reading period, as Marlene did. Cayce had discovered early on in the readings that he didn't have to know the person for whom he was reading, nor did they have to be present in the room with him. As long as he had the person's exact address or location at the time the reading was to be given, Cayce could read for people at great distances. However, the readings did say it was best if the person requesting the reading was present in the room.

Cayce had never seen the woman before, nor was his wife acquainted with her. Yet the Cayces rarely met a stranger, especially when people came for help through the readings. The psychic work had been a family business for thirty-five years, and the Cayces were comfortable with people from all walks of life.

Marlene, Gladys, and Gertrude were having a pleasant conversation prior to the reading period, and Cayce felt quite at home with Marlene. Cayce was able to perceive (psychically) that she was of a high, spiritual temperament. As he was "taking her in," a bizarre scenario suddenly unfolded in his field of vision: A ghostly apparition of a man appeared several feet off the floor behind Marlene. Cayce could see a man's body beginning to take form in the apparition. He saw the facial features perfectly; they were contorted in an expression of unbridled rage and hate. He had seen apparitions of the dead before, but something was terribly wrong with this one. The spirit of this man seemed to have the countenance of a demon. It was screaming at the woman in an agonized voice that only Cayce heard.

Too frightened to move or make a sound, Cayce

watched as the horrifying vision unfolded. He was shocked to see what appeared to be a knife clenched in the spirit's hand. The etheric figure, unseen by Gladys, Gertrude, or Marlene, moved forward quickly and brought the dagger down again and again, attempting to stab Marlene. The spirit howled in impotent rage as the knife passed harmlessly through her, his disembodied form unable to penetrate her physical body. Cayce watched the hideous spirit from another dimension attempt to attack and kill Marlene over and over again. Cayce quickly excused himself, rushed to the bathroom, closed the door, and vomited.

The most terrifying aspect of what Cayce had seen was that he knew in his heart that the vision of the maniacal spirit was, in some other dimension, real. Although Cayce was quite psychic in the conscious state, he couldn't see who the enraged spirit had been during life on earth, nor could he deduce why the spirit was intent upon harming Marlene.

Edgar realized the veil between the worlds of the living and dead was thin indeed, but he was thankful that discarnate entities were not able to do any harm to the living, such as Marlene's attacker was attempting to do. In that moment after witnessing the horrible scene, Edgar Cayce wished in earnest that he did not have the psychic ability to see through that veil.

Cayce gathered his shattered wits together and shook himself free of the shocking vision of the spectral monster. But he soon discovered that his vision was absolutely real. Marlene had written a letter to Gladys Davis prior to her arrival at the Cayce home, detailing a traumatic experience that shed light upon Cayce's nightmarish vision.

"In 1926, a terrible thing happened to me," Marlene had written. "I refused to marry a man whom I had been seeing. My mother was quite ill at the time and could not be left alone. I didn't feel it was fair to continue the relationship because of my family responsibilities. It was a hard decision."

When the man came to visit Marlene at her home, she gave him the news that their relationship must end, and she had to decline his proposal of marriage. Marlene did not realize that the man had become psychotically obsessed with her. Nor did she realize that the man had anticipated her decision. He appeared to understand, and he asked Marlene to join him on a drive through the country so they could have some last private moments together. After he drove a safe distance from Marlene's house in the woods, out of earshot of her family, he announced that if she wouldn't marry him, then she would marry no one. He parked the car in a secluded area. The man had an arsenal of weapons hidden in the car. He dragged Marlene from the car and beat her until she fell unconscious. He then stabbed her repeatedly. He shot her with a handgun. He bludgeoned her with a hammer, fracturing her skull. After he finished his grisly work, he assumed that Marlene was dead. He then picked up the handgun, placed it to his temple, and ended his own disturbed life.

"I was found three hours later by a man on horseback," Marlene wrote. "He rode home and called an ambulance. Attendants in the ambulance said I would never make it to the hospital."

Marlene was barely breathing when she was taken to the emergency room. Physicians who attended her in the hospital said she could not possibly live. That she was still breathing on her own at all by time the ambulance arrived at the hospital was miraculous. Marlene remembered very little of the ordeal.

"I remember he beat me unconscious," Marlene said.

"After that . . . just blackness. But I seem to recall hearing him calling my name from a far and distant place—somewhere in the blackness. I knew I couldn't go to him. I fought not to follow his voice—wherever he was, I'm not sure."[2]

Her last memory before losing consciousness was a strong sense of the will to live. After several lengthy surgeries to repair her skull, broken bones, and multiple stab and gunshot wounds, she slowly regained consciousness. Marlene awoke, surrounded by specialists and family members who knew they were witnessing a miracle. In time, Marlene's remarkable recovery was complete.

"After all these years, I've come to you, Mr. Cayce," Marlene said. "I just want to know why it happened to me, why I survived his attack, and what I should do with my life."[3] Reliving the ordeal was painful for Marlene, yet she felt some glimmer of hope from Edgar Cayce. She knew he had helped others in remarkable ways.

As she stood in the Cayces' living room nine years after the brutal attack, the only physical evidence of the trauma was a scar that ran along her left temple. Edgar Cayce now knew why he had perceived Marlene to be of a high spiritual temperament: She had returned from the dead. God certainly had moved in mysterious ways indeed, Cayce thought. The dark forces, however, also move in mysterious ways: The man who had killed himself was still in pursuit of Marlene from some strange, hellish place in the after-world. Perhaps it is a blessing that the majority of people cannot see the realms where some of the dead continue to live.

Cayce said nothing to Marlene about his psychic vision. However, prior to the reading, he called Gladys aside and confessed what he had witnessed in the spirit world. Edgar Cayce knew from his personal encounters with departed loved ones that in the realms of the dead, souls are not much different from their earthly existence. The body dies, consciousness takes a different form, but the essence of the soul does not change. The habits and patterns of the personality go with the departing soul. Marlene's tormented attacker had created, by his own malevolent motives and intentions, the very fabric of his afterdeath existence, chaining his soul to a hellish state of consciousness by his final deed.

"'As the tree falls, so does it lie . . . '" the sleeping Cayce had said in a psychic reading, paraphrasing Scripture. "For the beginnings in the next experiences [after death] are ever tempered by . . . the purpose . . . of the entity in the experience before." (5260-1)

Marlene's assailant was not freed by his suicide; he merely changed to a place where he was chained to his rage, malice, and horrible deeds. Thus, he hovered over the woman he once loved on earth, but could not reach or harm her.

Contrary to the grisly circumstances Cayce psychically perceived of the woman's life and near fatal attack, the reading he gave for her is spiritually inspiring. Cayce seemed to be speaking from a higher spiritual consciousness. The reading was encouraging:

> Keep that thou hast purposed, then, my child, in thine heart that [God's] ways may become that impelling force in the lives of those that meet thee day by day. Let those who look upon thy face take thought . . . that such glory, such beauty, such harmony, such oneness of light, *can only come from one who has been in the presence of Him that came unto His own* . . . [author's italics] 827-1

By surviving the bonds of death itself, Marlene stood

as a miraculous testament for many—her return to life bore the mark of the Divine. People who later came to meet her and learn her story were inspired, for her very survival was a miraculous thing indeed. In her life and existence, the Divine Force enabled her to carry on, survive, and prosper—defying even death itself.

The man who once loved Marlene existed within his own self-created hell on the other side. He would be freed only when he turned loose of his vengeance and hatred and sought the light. The free will every human being possesses in life continues after death. Only when the soul relinquishes its hold upon malice, hate, vengeance, and the things of the material world in order to embrace the light can the greater light come in. How quickly the process of leaving behind the material thoughts and desires after death goes is very much dependent upon how much spiritual consciousness is cultivated during the life on earth. Although the experience with Marlene was a frightening revelation to Edgar Cayce, it lent a clearer and sobering view of the worlds beyond death: that consciousness continues in its myriad forms just as it does on earth, even when that consciousness is evil.

These conscious revelations were the experiences that required Edgar Cayce to spend many of his waking hours alone. He often gardened and fished, and he walked several miles a day. He surrounded himself with a close circle of associates and his family. Cayce preferred to know nothing beforehand about the people who came for readings. He did not need many psychic visions such as he experienced with Marlene. The workings of Cayce's unconscious mind were as much a mystery to him as to people who came for readings. He didn't understand the powers he possessed anymore than they did. So he made up his mind early on that he would use what God had given him—consciously and unconsciously—to help the people closest to him and people who sought him out for psychic guidance. Cayce spent a great deal of time reading the Bible and in prayer. He prayed for the both the living and for the dead, for he understood that people such as the man who attacked Marlene could be released from an earthbound state of consciousness through the power of prayer.

George Ritchie saw for himself the realms in which people such as Marlene's attacker resided. Dr. Ritchie felt that most people who have near-death experiences are protected from seeing those realms because of the "tunnel" through which they pass.

"In talking with Raymond Moody," Ritchie said, "I was one of two cases [of near-death experiences] that did not have a 'tunnel effect.' I frankly feel that the tunnel is there to keep souls that are crossing over [upon physical death], from being subject to some very evil forces in the astral realms. I believe that is why people report seeing a tunnel that surrounds them as they head towards the Light. There are very bad forces, spirits that would try to distract them. It also protects the soul, immediately after death, from seeing the lower realms, the earthbound realms, the hellish realms. Of those realms, I was shown more of those than I cared to see."[4]

Many Americans, raised in households where traditional Christianity was the family religion, learned much more about hell and punishment than about the bliss of heaven and its rewards. According to the experiences of Dr. Ritchie, among others, the depths of hell and the heights of heaven are very real, and the soul will find itself—after death—somewhere in between those extremes, based upon the individual choices, will, and desires held while in the physical life. But the soul is not *sent* to those realms by some outside being or by God;

each soul creates its own after-death environment.

The question arose in Edgar Cayce's readings whether the soul can ever die. Cayce responded that the soul may be banished from the face of its Maker, but never die. This prompted the further question of the meaning of banishment. Cayce said it is the soul that chooses to remove itself from the Light and cast itself into the realms of utter darkness. At times, the soul may not be aware that it has made such a choice. It simply hangs on to the material consciousness after death instead of letting go. Hugh Lynn Cayce once described an event that frightened him very badly, where an earthbound spirit appeared to be standing in front of his bed for several nights in succession:

> I think this was the first experience I ever had with a so-called ghost. I was no more than five or six at the time. It happened while I was a child in Selma, Alabama. I would be sleeping in a room separated from Mom and Dad [Edgar and Gertrude Cayce]. I would wake up and find a woman standing at the foot of my bed, wringing her hands and crying. I could see her, but I could also see through her. I had this experience on several occasions. I would jump out of bed and run into the other room and jump in between my mother and father. The first two or three times they put up with this, but then Dad asked me what was wrong and I told him. He said, "Well, I'll take care of that. You won't see her any more." And I said, "That'll be fine. Then I'll be able to stay in bed." The woman never came back after that. Years later, when I asked Dad about it, he said that this had been the ghost of a woman who had become attached to that building because she had died there. He said he had actually seen her,

and he had explained to her what she should do and how she could release herself from being in that building.[5]

Edgar Cayce was able, through his clairvoyant ability, to communicate with the woman and tell her that she no longer needed to stay there; her work was complete. Perhaps she was wringing her hands and crying because she didn't know she had died, or she was distraught because she knew that she was caught "between the worlds." Edgar Cayce provided reassurance and gave her direction. A question about an experience similar to Hugh Lynn's was addressed in the readings. A woman who attended a spiritual study group in the Cayce home had a reoccurring experience of waking up in the night and seeing a deceased friend standing near her bed.

"From time to time," the woman said, "I have had come into my room a friend who has passed on. Is this contact harmful or beneficial?"

" . . . there are always those seeking that we may help," Cayce answered, "that may help us; for as we help another does help come to us. Pray for that friend, that the way through the shadows may be easier for them. It becomes easier for you." (262-25)

Dr. Ritchie witnessed earthbound planes of consciousness in his near-death experience. He saw realms where desperate souls were trapped by a passionate preoccupation with human and earthly affairs. He saw souls who held onto their material attachments and addictions after they had died. Regardless of what the individual's obsession had been in physical life—drinking alcohol, smoking, sexual addiction—all souls in these realms had one thing in common: All were fruitlessly attempting to satisfy the earthly passion to which they had become attached during physical life.

"What if one level of hell existed right here on the surface," Dr. Ritchie asked, "unseen and unsuspected by the living people occupying the same space? What if it meant remaining on earth but never again able to make contact with it . . . to want most, to burn with most desire, where you were most powerless—that would be hell indeed."[6]

Ritchie also saw a dimension of consciousness where souls were enraged and hate-filled. He saw the state of being through which souls such as Marlene's attacker passed at death:

> Now I saw there were other kinds of chains. These creatures [souls] seemed locked into habits of mind and emotion, into hatred, lust, destructive thought patterns . . . everywhere people were locked in what looked like fights to the death, writhing, punching, gouging . . . no weapons of any sort . . . only hands and feet and teeth . . . Although they appeared to be literally on top of each other, it was as though each man was boxing the air; at last I realized that of course, having no substance, they could not actually touch one another. They could not kill, though they clearly wanted to, because their intended victims were already dead . . . [7]

Although disturbing, those souls trapped in the hellish dimensions were not without hope, Dr. Ritchie said. Throughout his death experience, he observed angelic beings hovering above the earthbound souls, ever ready to help them be freed from their predicament—but the souls themselves had to willingly turn toward the light and request help to be freed—just as Edgar Cayce had described in his readings.

The next dimension Dr. Ritchie witnessed was quite disturbing:

I don't know where I was, but we were being
brought down into this large city—could have been
Los Angeles, or San Francisco, or New York or Chicago. All I know is that this city was near a large
body of water. We came down in front of this bar. I
could see the sailors, the marines, the soldiers, and
civilians going into this bar. But there were these
other beings there as well. The *human beings* I saw
had an electrical field or aura around them. When
the human beings in this bar got so intoxicated to
the point of about passing out, this electrical field
began to open from the top of the head downward.
And one of these other beings would come rushing,
trying to jump inside. It has taken me years to understand fully all the implications [of] my experience.[8]

The "other beings" that Dr. Ritchie spoke of were once
human but they had died. They all had one other thing
in common: All had been addicted to alcohol in their
earthly lives. After death, these souls couldn't move beyond their desire for alcohol. These "desire planes" of
consciousness chained the souls, even though no longer
incarnated, in an earthbound state. On each occasion
that someone lost consciousness in the bar, Dr. Ritchie
saw one of these souls, desperate to satisfy the desire for
alcohol, take possession for a brief few seconds, until the
human being came back to consciousness. Then the human body's aura closed again, and the earthbound spirit
was propelled out of the body.
Perhaps this explains why alcohol has such an adverse
effect on some people. The most well-mannered and
well-adjusted people can become violent, completely
changing in personality, while under the influence of alcohol. Is it possible that this complete change is, in actu-

ality, a form of possession from an earthbound soul? Dr. Ritchie wholeheartedly believes that it is not only possible, but probable.

The next dimension Dr. Ritchie was shown is particularly important and shows the consequences of how one's beliefs about the afterlife shape the immediate after-death environment of the soul. Dr. Ritchie said this realm was like a medical triage station at a hospital. All these souls were crossing over, and this was the "emergency room." The place was for determining where the souls who were crossing over should go for their future education and enlightenment:

> The first thing that I saw there were all the young soldiers, sailors, marines, civilians that were dying in 1943, during World War II. A lot of them were "crossing over." Tragically enough, a lot of them were like me—they had been taught that when you died you slept until Gabriel came along tooting on a horn. *Nothing could be further from the truth.* This [belief] has caused more trouble! And over there the angels were having a terrible time waking these young people up because they thought they had to stay asleep until the Second Coming of Christ.[9]

This closely parallels Cayce's reading that said many have remained what we would call dead for years, decades even, before realizing they were dead!

"I later realized," Dr. Ritchie added, "what they had so badly mixed up was St. Paul's writing in the fifteenth chapter of I Corinthians: 'In a moment, in the twinkling of an eye, at the last trump: for the trump shall sound, and the dead shall be raised incorruptible, and we shall be changed.' [I Corinthians 15:52] What nobody had taught me was [that the true meaning] of the 'last day' is *the last day you and I are here on this earth!* Not in some millennium later on, out here in space. The day you and I die is the day you and I are changed in the twinkling of an eye."[10] [author's italics]

The dimension of life immediately after death is known as the *astral* realm or what Cayce frequently called "the borderland." In this place, the dead are no longer attached to a physical body, but they are still very much in and around the material, earthly environment. At times the soul can be so enamored of its former life, that it will remain for some time—months, years, sometimes centuries—in the place where the soul once lived or died. The soul isn't "sentenced" to remain in astral realm for a set "time" period; time doesn't exist as we know it in those realms. Instead, the soul remains as long as it continues to focus its awareness and consciousness upon the earthly material world. In some cases, souls have remained in such a state for centuries.

Author and clergyman Canon J.D. Pearce-Higgins, vice president of The Churches' Fellowship for Psychical and Spiritual Studies in Great Britain, wrote extensively about his investigations into the psychic worlds. He chronicled many cases of earthbound spirits that haunted houses. In one particular case, Pearce-Higgins brought a medium to a site where strange apparitions and phenomena were happening. Once the medium went into trance, a dramatic tale spanning hundreds of years began to unfold:

> ... an ex-vicarage in the Midlands [was] haunted by two Tudor monks from the local priory, which had been dissolved at the Reformation. They were clearly a bad lot, one had made an Irish maid-servant pregnant; and the other had taken away and killed her baby. The girl herself through the medium

also spoke to us, pitifully saying, "Mistress Longhurst will not let me go out any more." Apparently Mistress Longhurst was her employer . . . The girl had been locked in an attic and finally poisoned after her baby had been despatched [sic]. She was still looking for her baby, unaware of its death and of the passage of time. The monks also had continued to perform their daily offices and although the Priory had been dissolved in A.D. 1536, still imagined themselves to be carrying out the daily monastic routine in field and church. I had a most interesting time trying to persuade them that they were dead, which they found hard to believe since they expected to sleep until the last trump and then, in virtue of their vows, to go straight to paradise or heaven. They could not understand at all where they were . . . All this had been previously accompanied by a long history over five years, from time to time, of heavy thumps in the attic, footsteps on the stairs, doors and the drawers paranormally opening and shutting, lights swinging to and fro; on two occasions eerie wailing cries, and the lady's dressing table shaking up and down in the middle of the night. Also there was often a heavy smell of pipe-smoking, though no-one in the house smoked. This was later found to be due to the presence of some old (spirit) tramps who had lived in the house while it was for some years derelict. Eventually the place was completely cleared.[11]

Think of the astonishment and difficulty the spirit guides on the other side have in rousing "sleeping" souls to the full awakening that there is no death. It behooves each one of us to reexamine our thoughts about the nature of the afterlife, for those thoughts not only go with us but determine where we go.

"Many souls wake up only gradually [after death]," Hugh Lynn Cayce said. "Many people who are attached to the earth, and who love the earth, love the things in the earth, whose appetites are strong in many different ways, are *tied to the earth*. And they're not aware that they have had a transition. It's just a gradual waking up."[12]

The waking-up process can be a difficult one—particularly if the death was premature, as in cases of suicide. Dr. Ritchie was shown a dimension of consciousness where souls indeed were "tied to the earth" as Hugh Lynn Cayce said, but they were tied because of their selfish desire to end their lives:

> The next realm I was shown was totally separated from that section that overlapped with the *human* beings. It was the realm of the suicides. I'm not speaking of suicide where a patient is psychotic, depressed, schizophrenic, or the type of people that Dr. Kevorkian is working on, where terminal illness is involved. I'm speaking of suicide of a nature that is the opposite of homicide: "If I can't kill you, I'll kill me to get even with you."[13]

Dr. Ritchie witnessed the abode of souls who killed themselves for revenge, spite, hate, resentment—purely selfish motives. "These beings became absolutely earthbound to the very people they had tried to hurt the most," he said. "They were tied to them until they realized the error of their ways."[14]

This "hell" was one of self-creation and was not an imposition or "sentence" doled out by God. The lesson, according to Ritchie, was that these beings would remain in this state until they fully realized that no soul has the right to kill another human being, including themselves.

The fundamental scientific principle of physics that matter can neither be created nor destroyed is even more true at a spiritual level, he said. And these souls, who in their misunderstanding had taken their own lives, were bound to the very people and circumstances they attempted to escape. A hellish realm, but not one that God ordained. By the human will to choose, these unfortunate ones had built their own world.[15]

The fundamental difference in what has popularly been taught about the concept of hell and what Dr. Ritchie saw is the *element of time*. In the earthbound realms, eternity is as long as the soul chooses to hold on to limited beliefs, hates, grudges, desires for vengeance, malice, etc. When the soul relinquishes these emotions, the guardian angels and spirits are then able to help the soul out of that realm, and it is no longer confined there. In more fundamentalist teachings, it is widely believed that the soul is banished to hell forever, without redemption. Cayce often said God has not willed that any soul should perish, but a means or way of escape is always available. It is up to the soul, however, to do the work of changing its consciousness, *changing its mind*, so that it can be free.

The next dimension after death that Dr. Ritchie was shown was like the place where Marlene's attacker would reside:

I thought by this time I'd seen it all, but not so. I was then taken to yet another realm I would not ever want to be in . . . without the Christ there beside me. I have never been in such a horrible place. The beings that inhabited this realm are full of hate, bitterness, resentment, bigotry and prejudice in a

manner you cannot imagine. Even in this realm
there were angels trying to get them to change their
minds. These beings, however, would prefer to try
to bludgeon one another to death, or commit some
bizarre sexual act . . . than leave.

No lake of fire and brimstone—something far
worse. Imagine being exposed to beings that are full
of hate and totally devoid of love. It was breaking
the heart of the Christ Himself. God doesn't send
anybody to hell. Those beings had put themselves
there by their own "stinking thinking," and deeds.[16]

What was particularly difficult for Dr. Ritchie to see
were the consequences of prejudicial thinking. For
people who had spent their lives holding onto their
prejudices—whether over color of skin, religious belief,
or sexual preference—there indeed was a corner of hell
reserved just for them. Dr. Ritchie blamed the existence
of such a dimension upon the misguided teachings of
churches, families, and communities. He said that to
learn to hate as much as he saw in these realms must be
deliberately taught. People are not born hating. Think,
for example, of a small rural town whose inhabitants are
staunchly prejudiced against a certain race or branch of
religion. Dr. Ritchie said these thoughts, carefully cultivated in a person over a lifetime create a dark and hellish
abode on the other side of death's door:

> I get very angry when I think about this realm. As
> a psychiatrist, when you've seen the number of sui-
> cides that I've seen because of some fundamental-
> ist religious teaching that has made the Devil more
> powerful than God, then you'll get angry, too. To
> hate all the people your relatives hated, you've got
> to be carefully taught. You have to be taught to be

afraid of people whose skin is a different color and whose eyes are different. You have to be carefully taught. And the *horror* it has let loose [over there] is almost indescribable. Those experiences in what I call hell, if I had any prejudices, [they were] shattered. I saw what kind of hell our prejudicial thinking, our thoughts about our fellow man, creates on the other side of this life. And we'd better change what we are teaching our children, our youth, and the prejudices we're getting across—and *quickly.*[17]

Just as there are both heavenly and hellish experiences on earth, there are gradients of the same after death—from the extremely harsh and hellish, to the dimly lit, to the brilliantly illuminated. These are metaphors for the dimensions of the soul's existence after death. One dimly lit dimension of life on this side is a shadow of limited beliefs in the afterlife itself. Frances Banks described, through Helen Greaves in *Testimony of Light,* her experiences in realms that she called "the land of the shadows":

. . . with Mother Florence's permission, [I have been] allowed to accompany her and some of the Sisters on their missionary work into the Shadowlands. It is a salutary experience. I am specially being instructed to recount the sad adventure to you . . . For it might be of use in clarifying the illusory ideas on the states of Heaven and Hell which have been fostered through the centuries . . . there are Heavens . . . there are spheres of unimaginable joy and beauty beyond, building up and extending out of every state of development, right on, I believe to the Spiritual Worlds of Divine Thought, far beyond any conception you and I have of them. Such is the progress of the soul towards these Spheres of Perfection and it is assuring to realize that we have all Eternity in which to journey onwards and "upwards."

But there are also hells . . . differing from the physical hells and everlasting fiery torments of man's warped imagination. There are hells of the spirit and the mind, confining states of misery; dark, depression and as real as the tortured consciousness of the dweller therein makes them. Yet these hells are not eternal. The man or woman in these mental torments need stay there no longer than his desires keep him. He is free to resist the hatreds, cruelties, lusts of his lower nature which he has retained from his earth life and which are keeping him in dark dungeons amid like-minded inhabitants . . . *No soul is ever left comfortless unless he wishes it . . .*

The Shadow Land is a very real place indeed; a gloomy murk covers it to which one has to become accustomed; squalid dwellings inhabited by unhappy, tormented beings who jeer and mock and pursue their warped existence. Sometimes these poor souls live in hatred and rebellion, sometimes in apathy and sometimes with a fierce denial that there is any other state of existence possible . . . [18]

For the many of us who have sought to find the purpose and meaning of life, the views of Frances Banks and Dr. Ritchie on the realms of heaven and hell place upon each soul great responsibility and offer endless opportunities for this life and the continued life after death: To the degree that we expand and learn and grow in love, grace, and wisdom, our souls will also grow to higher dimensions of love, grace, and wisdom after death. Likewise, we can see the consequences for narrow-mindedness, stubbornness, and refusal to learn love and forgiveness. There is no need for a judge or jury to weigh our sins in the afterlife: Our thoughts, beliefs, and actions *are* the judge and jury that bless us or damn us according to what we have done with life's opportunities.

A unique book was published in the early 1950s that further sheds light upon these concepts. *The Boy Who Saw True* is a posthumously published series of journals that document the life of a psychically gifted child. Like Edgar Cayce, the boy grew up consciously psychic, and he was befuddled because he didn't understand why the rest of his family couldn't see his dead grandfather, who acted as the boy's guardian angel. The boy began keeping the journal in 1885, and in a child's language, he chronicled the relationships with people who were living and dead. His recorded clairvoyant visions documented some of the finest material on the afterlife, discarnate spirits, life after death, and the nature of the transition from physical life to the soul's existence after death. The boy consciously saw and communicated with the dead and relayed the conversations to his mentor and tutor, Mr. Patmore, who took verbatim notes of the dialogues.

In one dialogue, the boy was talking with his dead grandfather, and he inquired about his grandmother and why the two of them were no longer together as they were in the physical world:

> I asked him [the grandfather] why grandmamma never came to see us too. And he said something about spirits getting thought-bound like birds getting egg-bound, and made us all laugh because it seemed such a funny thing to say. He told us that while the grandmater [sic] was still on earth, she

reckoned, same as a lot of people do, that she and a few other people were going to be saved. "And now," said Grandpa, "she lives in a world of thoughts which she and others have created by their own fallacious convictions. In our Father's house are many mansions."[19]

The grandmother was in a thought-form dimension where she literally was singing hymns around a large throne with others of like-mind. If any spirit guides or angels came to try to get them to ascend to a higher dimension of consciousness, the grandmother and the others would scream in horror, presupposing that the visiting spirit was a demon or someone sent from hell. She believed this because only those in her realm were the souls who were "saved." The rest of the world, in their belief, had been sent to hell!

When we asked Grandpa, what about him, he said, though he had believed in God and all that, he'd never made up his mind too much what the other world was going to be like, so now he didn't spend his life singing hymns round an imaginary throne of God like Grandma does . . . He told us Grandma had been an obstinate old woman, and she was still obstinate now, and nothing he could say was going to change her (outlook) till she got sick of it and began looking round for something better. He told us it was a great mistake to have preconceived notions like my late lamented grandmother; but seeing as I didn't know what he meant, I asked Mr. Patmore, who says it's if people are too cock sure of a thing when they've nothing proper to go on . . . [20]

The boy and his private tutor, Mr. Patmore, chronicled the case of an earthbound soul. While Patmore and the boy were visiting an old castle in Wales, the child became aware of a spirit who was standing nearby and alerted Patmore. The following is a transcript of a conversation they held with a spirit who could not believe that he was dead:

The spirit who turned up was that old friend of Mr. P's [Patmore] . . . The first thing he said was "Hello, Patmore. Fancy seeing you here." Then Mr. P asked who he was. And [the friend] said, "What a question." . . . He was surprised Mr. P didn't recognize him. So Mr. P was very surprised too, and said he was blowed [sic], but that of course he couldn't recognize him because he couldn't see people who were dead . . . And now I'll write what Mr. P gave me for dictation . . . Mr. Patmore says I can put P for Patmore and C for Cliff [the discarnate spirit] so as to save time.

C: What are you writing there?
P: I'm writing down what you say.
C: What the devil for?
P: Because I want to remember what you tell us.
C: What nonsense.
P. Not at all, I'm interested. I'm very pleased you have come. But what gave you the idea?
C: I like the place, and wanted to see it again. It was I who told you about these rooms.
P: Yes, I know you did. Tell me, how are you feeling?
C: I never felt better in my life, physically, but mentally—well, I seem to be a bit confused. It's damn queer.
P: You used to be an Agnostic. I suppose you've altered your views now?

C: Of course I haven't. Why should I?

P: Because you must know there's an after-life now.

C: I don't know anything of the kind, and don't believe any of the people who tell me all that nonsense. Who is this young lad, by the way, and why does he have to repeat to you everything I say?

P: Because he can see you and hear you, and I can't.

C: Have you gone blind and deaf?

P: Of course not. But you are now a spirit, and I can't see spirits.

C: I am not a spirit. I don't believe in spirits and I never have.

P: But surely you can't think you are still on this earth? Can't you remember what happened?

C: I remember feeling infernally ill. Then I lost consciousness and after that I woke up feeling better than ever.

P: Yes, and then what happened?

C: Look here, Patmore, I resent all this interrogation and your writing down everything I say like a policeman.

P: Sorry, my dear Cliff, but I'm very much interested. You don't appear to realize that you are what we down here call dead, though I appreciate the fact that you feel very much more alive.

C: There's no "down here" about it. You talk as if I were standing on a cloud and you were below. I never heard such rubbish. The only thing that's the matter with me is that sometimes my sight and hearing seem a bit queer.

P: You mean perhaps that we look a bit dim to you and sound rather far off?

C: Yes, in a sense.

P: That's because you are a spirit and we have still got physical bodies.

C: I refuse to believe that I am a spirit. There are no spirits. When we die that is the end of us. You annoy me. You always did annoy me when we got talking on this subject, because you will not face facts. You can't get round science, and science declares that we have evolved from monkeys. I'm going. I've had enough of this futile argument. We shall never convince one another, so what's the good of talking? Good-bye.

When he'd cleared out, Mr. Patmore pulled a funny face and said he hadn't changed a bit and always went on like that when he was alive. He said Mr. Cliff had been taken ill in the street and had died · in a hospital . . . [21]

The time it takes for the soul to adjust and adapt from the physical environment to its environs after death varies; there is no formula for what constitutes that which is normal or abnormal. Each individual adapts and comprehends knowledge and understanding at his or her own pace and time frame in the earth. Just so, the orientation process after death is also an individual experience. For example, the deceased grandfather of the boy had no hard and set belief systems about would happen after death. Because of his openness, he adapted more readily to the after-death environment. His grandmother, however, held onto a set of dogmatic beliefs about the afterlife, and they formed her existence (i.e., singing songs around the "imaginary throne of God"). Because she believed that was all there was, she had bound herself to a limited dimension of consciousness after death. Only by opening her mind and discarding her current set of beliefs would the grandmother be able to gravitate to the higher dimensions. Other people, like Patmore's friend Cliff, who staunchly refused to believe

there was *anything* after death, find themselves disoriented. They wander aimlessly through the earthbound
realms, fruitlessly attempting to communicate with
those still physically alive. They can't understand why no
one can see or hear them. It is only after they grow weary
and fall deeper into disillusionment that they finally relinquish their stubborn denial about life after death. At
that critical point, the soul will pray for help, and immediately their guardian spirits or angels can assist them
out of the earthbound realms. Hugh Lynn Cayce summed
up the importance of mentally and spiritually preparing
for death by using an interesting metaphor:

> If you were going to go on an expedition to the
> Yucatan, you would prepare yourself by getting a
> map. You would find out the appropriate clothing
> to wear. Before the trip even began, you would
> study and educate yourself about the culture, the
> climate, dangers, and pitfalls to be wary of, as well
> as map out the historic sites you'd want to see.
> Preparation for such a journey is good common
> sense. Apply that philosophy to your eventual jour
> ney through the death transition. Closely examine
> what your thoughts and desires are creating. It
> makes good common sense to map out your jour
> ney *before* you go. That way, you won't get lost on
> the way to the Light.[22]

Edgar Cayce said:

> ... each soul is a portion of creation, and builds
> ... through its physical-mental or spiritual-mental,
> [the experience] it has builded for itself. And each
> entity's heaven or hell must, through *some* experience,
> be that which it has builded for itself ... 281-16

9

Preparing for Life
in the Next World

*. . . a death in the flesh is a birth into the realm of another
experience, to those who have lived in such a manner as not to
be bound by earthly ties.*   Edgar Cayce Reading 989-2

*W*hen the American mass media began reporting accounts of near-death experiences, communications between the living and the dead, and extrasensory perception, the Western world made its first tentative steps toward a more enlightened worldview about the nature of the soul and spirit. The magazine articles, television documentaries, and numerous books written on these subjects have helped usher humanity into an era of spiritual renaissance. The illuminating stories of near-death survivors and the reassuring accounts of loved ones who have visited the living have helped move us a step closer to the light of understanding and away from the shadows of fear about death and dying.

For eons we have been taught to fear. Sects of fundamentalist Christian religions have taught people to fear God. We have been taught to be afraid of the life after death because many of us believed we were going straight to hell in a handbasket, without any hope of redemption. In light of the thousands of accounts of near-death experiences documented by Dr. Raymond Moody, these teachings appear to be nothing more than misconceptions. The majority of NDE survivors Dr. Moody interviewed *knew* without any doubt that they were loved without condition by a force greater than themselves—God. They knew they were an integral part of this universal source of love. This powerful sense of love, they said, was not dependent upon anything they did or said—it simply was a *fact of consciousness*. The most important lesson they learned from dying was that their purpose in life was to go about the business of loving others unconditionally just as they themselves were loved. Dr. Moody said if every human being on earth acted on that simple principle of unconditional love, then we could truly have a heaven on earth.

This message of love is perhaps the most important facet of knowledge that has come out of NDE research. The extent of our spiritual growth, development, and evolution—in this world as well as in the next—is measured and is dependent upon our willingness to manifest unconditional love towards our fellow human beings.

The time-honored saying that when someone has died they have "passed on to their reward" is very much a valid truth. Each person inherits or is "rewarded" with the sum total of what they have built during their physical lives. According to Edgar Cayce, we are constructing the state of consciousness we will move into after death by our thoughts, desires, intentions, and deeds in the material world. If we consciously seek to act from an intention of love and to manifest compassion, love, forgiveness, patience, etc., these spiritual virtues literally create for us the "reward" of a light-filled existence after death. It isn't on the merit of *accomplishment* that we move to the higher realms after death; it is from loving and acting from the heart, from a place of spiritual understanding in all facets of our lives. What we have cherished in our hearts and minds will have a great deal to do with where we find ourselves after death.

As Dr. Ritchie illustrated, the souls that find themselves in the shadowlands or the earthbound realms after death are not being punished or condemned by any force or power except of their own making. The *inner life* creates the *outer world* of our existence after death. If we have spent a lifetime holding grudges, harboring resentments, being prejudicial in our thinking, acting out of jealousy or hate or malice, those thoughts collectively form the building blocks that create a home in the shadowlands, the hellish realms. In accordance with universal law, that which we think, we become; that which we build, we move into. Edgar Cayce's answer to a question posed to him in a reading defines the workings of this universal law in short order:

(Q) Where do I go from this planet?
(A) Where thou art preparing, and what thou art building. 1219-1

How can we best prepare and build for ourselves a light-filled existence after we leave this world? How can we build a consciousness that far transcends the trappings of the earthbound realms after death? Hugh Lynn

Cayce offered his insights during a question-and-answer session at one of his lectures:

> The actual preparation lies in prayer, in medita-
> tion, in looking for the light, and in recognizing your
> goals, plans, desires, and purposes—the things that
> you want to get done, as well as those you have al-
> ready accomplished—all are part of the whole, and
> you are going to go right on moving toward them in
> another dimension. The transition involves a change
> of body, but you just walk through the door and you
> keep on doing things. You do them a little faster [af-
> ter death], and you do them in another dimension,
> but you are carrying on what you have planned,
> what you desired, what you thought about; you
> continue doing the things you started doing on this
> side and you move right along with them. You are
> moving toward the ideals, goals, and purposes that
> you have set . . . [1]

Hugh Lynn also added that if we want to find our way to the Light after death, we need to be able to find and recognize the Light here, during our time on earth. We can begin to expand our beliefs and increase our knowledge and understanding about the eternal nature of life through study and through reading, but one of the most important avenues to true spiritual understanding is through working with dreams. As was stated in previous chapters, Hugh Lynn believed that recording dreams provides a picture of the realm we will pass to after physical death:

> There is material in the Edgar Cayce readings that
> explains how dreams are [a way] of viewing the
> thought forms that we have created; and so, if we

can see our dreams carefully detailed, we are actually seeing the world of thought forms into which we will move when we die. If we can become familiar with the dream world, we will be immediately familiar with the world we move into [after physical death], and it will not seem so strange to us at all. It is like a dream world, and it changes very rapidly, just as dreams change with our thoughts. Now, as I understand the readings, in working with dreams—particularly dreams that indicate movements of groups of people in houses or places—we are actually dealing with our thought forms. They are worlds or creations of our own minds, and they are very real for the person who passes over . . . I urge people to pray for an understanding of where they will be going, and I suggest that they ask to be shown the kind of world into which they will move . . . [2]

As we begin to grow in spiritual awareness, applying principles that magnify the Spirit in our daily lives, we move to a higher state of consciousness in the waking state as well as in our dream state. Many people say they don't remember their dreams. The Cayce readings say that if little attention is paid to dreams, there will be little or no recall. However, once we begin to take an interest in remembering and studying dreams, within a short period of time dream recall improves. Cayce gave an important reading on this subject in 1939:

. . . have ye not wondered why in the sacred writings it is said that God no longer spoke to man in visions and dreams? It is because man fed not his soul, his mind, upon things spiritual; thus closing the avenue or channel through which God might speak with the children of men. For, only they who believe He *is* may make manifest that as a reality in their experience through the material sojourns. 1904-2

In other words, if we believe that dreams are an avenue through which we can communicate with the Creator, then the channel opens for us to receive information and guidance through dreams. Through working and making a record of our dreams, we can grow in spiritual awareness, communicate with deceased loved ones, and help "build" a higher consciousness for ourselves after death. As we seek to broaden our consciousness in this world, we naturally broaden our consciousness for our eventual advent into the next.

A very practical way we can begin to work with dreams is through the art of *dream incubation*. This practice combines the disciplines of both prayer and spiritual dreamwork. Incubating a dream involves consciously posing a question or statement before going to sleep in order to receive the answer or guidance through a dream. To begin this practice, simply keep a pad of paper and a pen close to your bedside. If you have had little or no recollection of dreams for a long period of time, simply write down the following statement three times on your pad or dream journal: "I will remember my dreams upon awakening," and then concentrate upon the desire to do so. When you awaken in the night or in the morning, write down your dream recollections. Don't become frustrated if you don't recall any dreams for the first week or two. Some people begin to remember their dreams after a few days of writing the suggestion; for others, it may take a couple of weeks. After you begin to remember your dreams on a regular basis, then do the dream incubation exercises that begin on page 182.

Seeking to obtain guidance and direction through

dreams is like working with prayer. The written statement or question you ask before going to sleep is like a letter to the Creator. You are asking for divine guidance, understanding, and help. Approach dream incubation with a sense of reverence and sacredness. As Cayce said, God will speak directly to the individual; we only need to have faith and hold the belief that such experiences are possible.

With that in mind, the following three exercises are for three specific areas with which you may need spiritual assistance. Feel free to use your own words in forming the written dream incubation statement, or copy the examples below. Work with each of these for thirty consecutive days and nights. Before you go to bed each night, read over the dreams you recorded from the previous night and write down any ideas or feelings you have about them. As you drift off to sleep, focus upon your *desire* and *expect* to receive a dream that will give you the information you need. The desire and expectancy help open the avenue of the subconscious for the conscious mind to receive clear guidance in the morning.

As you begin to have dreams, don't become confused by attempting to interpret the symbology of the dreams you have—simply write them down. At the conclusion of thirty days, go back through and read your recorded dreams. Look at the *activity* of each dream. Examine what you are were *doing* in it. The message of dreams is often contained not in the symbols themselves, but in your *actions* and the actions of people around you. The other people in your dreams often represent a facet of your self. On the other hand, if you are seeking to have closure with a deceased loved one, and that person appears in your dream, it is probable that you are in communion with that loved one. The Cayce readings say that when we dream of a deceased loved one, it is, more times than not, a *real* contact.

As Hugh Lynn said, dreams are an avenue through which we can transcend the conscious mind and become aware of the after-death dimensions. The more accustomed we become to our dreams and the greater awareness we gain through dream study, the more we gain in awareness here during our physical lives, and the more we become familiar with the dimensions that we pass to after physical death.

Dream Incubation Exercises

1. *Dream incubation for healing bereavement and communicating with a deceased loved one*—As you get ready to go to sleep, have a brief period of prayer or meditation and ask that you be divinely guided in your quest. Then, write down the following dream incubation statement three times:

> Please help me understand through my dreams the continuity of life after death, and help me to know that [the deceased person] is alive and well on the other side. If it is in keeping with divine will, and will be helpful for each, I request that I may communicate with [the deceased person]. Thank you. I will remember my dreams. I will remember my dreams. I will remember my dreams.

Before you go to sleep, say a prayer for the soul of the deceased friend or relative about whom you are asking guidance. See that person surrounded in white light, and request that you be divinely guided during your sleep state to obtain healing for yourself and to help bring light and healing to the soul who has passed on.

2. Dream incubation experiment to understand the oneness of life and death—As you get ready to go to sleep, have a brief period of prayer or meditation and ask that you be divinely guided in your quest. Then, write down the following dream incubation statement three times:

Please help me to better understand the continuity of life through my dreams. Please direct me through my dreams to find and recognize the Light, that I may be a channel of blessings to those in this world and in the next. Thank you. I will remember my dreams. I will remember my dreams. I will remember my dreams.

Remember, the soul-mind has within it all answers to any questions that may be asked; we only need to attune our finite conscious minds to that unlimited spiritual resource of knowledge. The more aware we become in our dream state—and a *conscious* state of awareness can be attained through working with dreams—the more aware we will be at the death transition. The state of sleep and dreams is directly linked, according to Edgar Cayce, to the state of consciousness after death.

In his book, *The Tibetan Book of Living and Dying,* Sogyal Rinpoche detailed the Buddhist concept that the realms of dreams and the realms after death are one. Rinpoche used the Tibetan word *bardo* to describe various transitory levels of consciousness the soul passes through during and after physical death and during sleep and dreams. Becoming familiar with the bardos through dreamwork is beneficial to the soul here and hereafter because such spiritual understanding will help us find the Light after death:

Of course the bardos of death are much deeper

states of consciousness than the sleep and dream states . . . but their relative levels of subtlety correspond and show the kind of links and parallels that exist between all different levels of consciousness. Masters often use this particular comparison to show just how difficult it is to maintain awareness during the bardo states. How many of us are aware of the change in consciousness when we fall asleep? Or of the moment of sleep before dreams begin? How many of us are aware even when we dream that we are dreaming? . . . How your mind is in the sleep and dream state indicates how your mind will be in the corresponding bardo states; for example, the way in which you react to dreams, nightmares, and difficulties now shows how you might react after you die. This is why the yoga of sleep and dream plays such an important part in the preparation for death. What a real practitioner seeks to do is to keep, unfailing and unbroken, his or her awareness of the nature of the mind throughout the day and night, and so use directly the different phases of sleep and dream to recognize and become familiar with what will happen in the bardos during and after death.[3]

Author and psychotherapist G. Scott Sparrow has conducted personal and professional dream research for many years. He says that everyone has the capacity to become *lucid* in the dream state (the awareness that one is dreaming while in the dream). From that heightened state of awareness, we have the capacity to transcend the bardos and consciously experience a deep sense of communion with the all-loving, all-powerful Light that others have contacted in their near-death experiences. Communion with the Light (which represents the

Source of all life, God) is at the heart of every person's spiritual search. The Cayce readings indicate that such a state of communion is the birthright of every soul, that all creatures have the right to consciously commune and become one with the Creator. As we hold to this thought in working with dreams, we can be assured that the spiritual art of dream incubation will bring us closer to that conscious awareness. That which we develop in this world will go with us when we leave the physical body behind at physical death.

Working with a form of daily meditation is a powerful spiritual practice that can help immensely in understanding the continuity of life. Meditation helps awaken the soul-mind, the part of us that can never die, and that divine wisdom can flow in and through us and help process the grief that naturally accompanies the loss of a close friend or loved one. We can intellectually *know* that the soul continues after physical death, but that intellectual knowledge doesn't quell the feelings of loss. Meditation helps us to comprehend spiritual truths in an entirely different way from our intellectual, reasoning mind. The intellect uses only the faculties of reason, conceptualization, and interpretation to translate our experiences into a mental framework of understanding. It doesn't help when the heart is breaking because someone close to us has died. We must go to the deeper levels of ourselves in order to receive the healing we need. The soul-mind *experiences* and *understands* spiritual principles through unfoldment and expansion of consciousness. The conscious mind has the ability to expand in order to become aware of its soul mind and experience the reality of the unseen dimensions that transcend the boundaries of time and space. Meditation is a powerful tool to move beyond the conscious mind's beliefs and enter a realm where it can *experience divine wisdom and unfoldment.* In the silence of the inner self, we can come to comprehend the eternal nature of the soul. Edgar Cayce said:

> Death ... may not be understood by the third dimensional mind from the third dimensional analysis *but must be seen from the fourth dimensional force as may be experienced by an entity gaining ... the insight* and concept of such phenomenized conditions, see? [author's italics] 136-18

It has been said that, in prayer, we speak to God, while through meditation, we *listen.* Cayce gave an outline that described why meditation is important and how it can help everyone live a well-rounded, balanced spiritual life:

> [Meditation] is the attuning of the physical and mental attributes seeking to know the relationships to the Maker. *That* is true meditation. For ye must learn to meditate, just as ye have learned to walk, to talk ... Then, there must be a conscious contact between that which is part of thy body-physical, thy body-mental, to thy soul-body, or thy superconscious. 281-41

Rinpoche wrote:

> The purpose of meditation is to awaken in us the sky-like nature of the mind and to introduce us to that which we really are, our unchanging pure awareness, which underlies the whole of life and death. In the stillness and silence of meditation, we glimpse and return to that deep inner nature that we have so long ago lost sight of amid the busyness

and distraction of our minds . . . We don't know who
we really are, or what aspects of ourselves we
should identify with or believe in. So many contra-
dictory voices, dictates, and feelings fight for control over our inner lives that we find ourselves
scattered everywhere, in all directions, leaving nobody at home. Meditation, then, is bringing the
mind home.[4]

There are many techniques and approaches to meditation. The technique isn't of great importance; the desire and intention to commune with the Creator are of
utmost importance. Rinpoche believes that each meditation is an opportunity to dedicate one's self and one's
life to the unfoldment and enlightenment of self and
others. Before each meditation, Rinpoche offers the following prayer, which he says all buddhas of the past have
prayed:

> By the power and truth of this practice:
> May all beings have happiness, and the causes
>   of happiness;
> May all be free from sorrow, and the causes of
>   sorrow;
> May all never be separated from the sacred
>   happiness which is sorrowless;
> and may all live in equanimity, without too
>   much attachment and too much aversion,
> And live believing in the equality of all that
>   lives.[5]

It is in that spirit that every person should approach
meditation. When we experience peace within, a sense
of communion, a lessening of the grief, then that experience is a light that shines through us and raises the vi-

brations of both the souls in the earth and those who have passed on. We are intricately connected to a divine source, and we are intricately connected to one another. So, when we enter into meditation, we are attuning to the entire universe. In the inner sanctuary of our selves, according to Edgar Cayce, we will find a peace that is beyond description.

Here is a simple, step-by-step method that outlines the meditation process. This approach is based on the Edgar Cayce readings:

- Cleanse the body with pure water.
- Sit or lie in a comfortable position.
- Focus your attention on your breath; breathing deeply and evenly. Breath is life, and so as you breathe in, feel that you are breathing in life itself. With each exhalation, imagine that you are letting go of all pain, all concerns, all worries. Imagine yourself sitting in a very serene, very peaceful place, surrounded by a brilliant, protective white Light. See and feel this light both surrounding you and entering into you with every breath you take.
- Ask that you be divinely guided and protected as you enter into meditation. A prayer of protection is helpful because in meditation you are opening yourself to many unseen forces and beings. As you say a prayer of protection, focusing on your highest spiritual aspirations, ideals, and intentions, you can be sure there will be no interference from lesser developed or mischievous spirit entities that dwell in the lower astral, earthbound realms.

Edgar Cayce said:

> . . . know that if ye surround yourself with the creative forces or vibrations that are the way, the truth and the light, then *only* good may come; and those

things of dire natures, or demoniacal forces in any form will not be a part of thy experience. 2539-2

The following is an example of a prayer that can be used as a prayer of protection before entering into meditation:

As I open myself to the Unseen Forces that surround the Throne of grace, beauty and might, I surround myself with the pure white Light of protection that is found in the thought of Christ [God, Allah, One Spirit, etc.]. I seek only that the will of the Most High be done in me, and through me, just now. Amen.

As you say these words aloud or silently, see yourself infused with the light, and realize that you are entering into meditation so that you can commune with the Source of all light, all love. Holding that thought in mind will help silence the "noise" of the conscious mind and alleviate distractions.

Edgar Cayce gave a breathing exercise that is helpful in attuning the body, mind, and spirit to the Source. After saying the prayer of protection, perform the following breathing exercises three times each: Close off your left nostril, and breathe deeply through the right. As you inhale, imagine you are breathing in *strength*. Exhale slowly through the mouth. After doing this three times, close off the right nostril, inhale deeply through the left, and imagine you are breathing in *light*. Exhale slowly through the right nostril. Again, these are only suggestions. Feel free to approach meditation in any way you wish.

Many people use a chant prior to meditating. Chanting helps in the attunement process and helps open the doorway to the higher states of consciousness. The following chant was given in the Cayce readings as an aid to further deepen the attunement process in meditation. Take in a very deep breath, sound out the chant very slowly, and hold the last part of the chant (OM) as long as possible. As you perform this chant, imagine yourself being filled with light, love and peace. Do this three times in succession:

Arrrr—eeeee—OM (it sounds like "r - e - o - mmm").

After repeating the chant, then return to focusing on your breath. You will notice that the conscious mind is very quiet and very still. Try to remain in the silence of meditation by focusing on a phrase or word that helps keep you centered during the meditation. It may be something such as, "I am with you always," or, "I will bring all things to your remembrance," or "I am now at peace in the presence of God." When your conscious mind becomes distracted or preoccupied by outside thoughts, gently bring your attention back to the words or phrase that you've chosen, and repeat them aloud if necessary. Above and beyond anything else, *relax* and just allow yourself to *rest* in the quietude of your inner self.

As you practice regular meditation every day, it isn't unusual to have psychic experiences both while meditating and during conscious awareness. The people who took part in Edgar Cayce's study group program in the 1930s and '40s, and worked with daily meditation had many visionary and illuminating experiences.[6] Some discovered the ability to heal others. Others developed the ability to communicate with angels or deceased loved ones. Some learned to interpret dreams. Meditation opens the doorway for the conscious self to unfold and become aware of itself as a spiritual being. With this unfoldment, according to the readings, the sixth, or psychic, sense is naturally awakened.

A woman came to Cayce and asked in a reading about a light experience she had after meditation. Cayce told her:

> This followed a deep meditation . . . it has not entered the heart of man all the glories that have been prepared, nor all the beauties that may be experienced by those that seek His face. These are but signs, yea the *assurances*, that His presence abideth with thee. Know He hath promised that if ye ask, ye shall receive. Be satisfied only then with the consciousness of His presence . . . For "If ye will knock, I will open—for I stand at the door and knock." If ye will but open thy tabernacle of consciousness to allow the holy to come in and sup with thee, yea *all* the beauties of peace and harmony *are* thine; for they are the birthright of each soul. For the soul is the portion of the Maker that makes thee individual, yet the consciousness of being one with *God*, the *universe*, the *love*—that which *is* beauty and harmony . . . That awakening . . . is coming. More and more as the white light comes to thee, more and more will there be the awakening . . . 987-4

Hugh Lynn Cayce had many powerful experiences in meditation throughout his lifetime. And, as his father had recommended, he took such experiences as assurances that he was on the right track, heading closer in consciousness to the eternal Light.

"If you have a vision of a deceased loved one, or have an experience of seeing Jesus," Hugh Lynn said, "acknowledge the being, receive their message, and then go right back to meditating. These experiences come as signs along the way . . . Also remember that each time you meditate, you are building the light body that you will move into after physical death. The more you can find that Light in meditation, the closer you get to a conscious communion with the Maker, then you will advance that much faster after physical death."[7]

At the end of a meditation period, a great deal of energy has been raised in the body, whether we are aware of it or not. Some people get a feeling of heat or warmth after meditation especially through the hands or forehead. This energy that has been raised is healing energy. The readings strongly recommended that this energy be sent out in prayer to give healing to others—both those who are living and those who are dead. Imagine a flood of light and energy coming in through the top of your head, infusing and filling your body, mind, and soul. This is what happens in meditation, and that energy is a living force; it needs to move *through* us. Prayer after meditating is the best way to send it out to other living individuals, to souls who have passed on, and to the world. At the close of your meditation, give thanks for the opportunity for communion with the Divine and ask to be used as a channel of blessings and hope to the people you meet in all walks of life.

Meditation is the gateway to bringing the dormant spiritual self into the conscious mind and into waking life. In the Bible, Jesus said to His disciples that the Holy Spirit would come and "shall teach you all things, and bring to your remembrance whatsoever I have said unto you." (John 14:26) Cayce's readings indicated that this is a *literal promise*; and that through meditation and prayer, the soul-mind can become so awakened that we indeed have the potential to attain to a state of divine wisdom and remembrance of *all things*. Just as Cayce became attuned to the infinite Source of universal knowledge, we too have that same ability because we are eternally linked, at the soul level, with all souls and the Source of all life, God:

... drawing nigh unto the Father-God (within) ye may become more and more aware of thy purposes for being here. For His promise is to bring to thy remembrance all those things from the foundations of the earth! 1567-2

Meditation also helps accelerate the healing process, particularly when we are bereaved over the death of a loved one. Cayce said the questions many of us seek to know—the whys for a person dying young or someone's unexpected death—cannot be explained in the framework of the three-dimensional world. *We must enter into the silence of ourselves* so that we can commune with the Most High and receive divine knowledge and healing that are beyond the reaches of the finite, material world. By entering into the silence of ourselves, we can comprehend and *experience* the divine order of all things in a manner beyond words and explanation, beyond the *reasoning, conscious mind.* As long as we seek to find answers to questions outside of ourselves, searching for rational or intellectual answers in the world, we will find nothing but confusion and come away from our search empty-handed.

Rinpoche said in his book that seeking for spiritual answers in the material world naturally leads to a great deal of confusion because our modern society specializes in distractions that lead human beings away from the real truth about their spiritual nature:

Modern society seems to be a celebration of all the things that lead away from the truth, make truth hard to live for, and discourage people from even believing that it exists. And to think that all this springs from a civilization that claims to adore life, but actually starves it of any real meaning; that end-

lessly speaks of making people "happy," but in fact
blocks their way to the source of real joy. This modern *samsara* feeds off an anxiety and depression
that it fosters and trains us all in, and carefully nur-
tures with a consumer machine that needs to keep
us greedy to keep us going . . . it assaults us from
every angle with its propaganda, and creates an almost impregnable environment of addiction around
us . . . As the eighteenth-century Tibetan master
Jikme Lingpa said, "Mesmerized by the sheer variety of perceptions, beings wander endlessly astray
in samsara's vicious cycle."[8]

Everything in this physical world is temporary and
passing. A state of enlightenment can be attained by
turning from the *samsara*—the world of distractions and
illusions—to the heart and inner spirit where truth resides. It is only by the soul's seeking for itself that true
spiritual understanding and revelation can occur. The
outer world holds no comprehensive answers to our
lives, our death, and what lies beyond. So the search for
the meaning of life and an understanding of death must
be found within. Moving beyond the sense of grief and
loss after the death of a loved one can be accomplished
by seeking the silence and peace of the inner worlds
through meditation, prayer, and working with dreams.

Rinpoche said an important part of understanding the
oneness of life and death is by consciously contemplat-
ing the reality of our own eventual death:

It is important to reflect calmly, again and again,
that *death is real and comes without warning*. Don't
be like the pigeon in the Tibetan proverb. He spends
all night fussing about, making his bed, and dawn
comes up before he has even had time to go to

sleep. As an important twelfth-century master, Drakpa Gyaltsen, said, "Human beings spend all their lives preparing, preparing, preparing . . . Only to meet the next life unprepared."[9]

We can be better prepared to leave this world if we follow this guidance. If we strive to live our lives focused on being more compassionate, loving, and forgiving to the people in our daily lives, and as we work with the spiritual disciplines of prayer, meditation, and dreamwork, then we are taking important steps in preparing ourselves for the next phase of our lives after physical death. The light that we find and commune with during meditation, the light that we experience in our dreams, will be our guide even if our death comes early or unexpectedly. We won't be caught unprepared or unaware. At the point of the death transition, the all-loving, all-powerful Light is there for each and every soul. Whether the soul is able to see that Light and is able to move toward it is a matter of individual development. During a lecture presentation, Hugh Lynn Cayce described a case that illustrates the consequences of being ill-prepared for death:

> Years ago, when my family was in Selma, Alabama, I was party to a strange experience. A man who was considered a miser lived across the street from us. He was a grumpy old gentleman who worked in the cotton exchange and was supposed to have had a lot of money. We *heard* him die. He had big strong doors on his apartment and they couldn't break them down. They had to call the fire department and climb in the window. He was screaming horribly, but he died before the rescuers could reach him—it was pretty bad. [Eleven years later] Dad was giving a reading on someone in

Selma, Alabama, and near the end of the reading, he named the same gentleman I had heard die as a child and said, "This man has just become aware that he is dead!" Those who are attached to the earth, who love the things in the earth, and whose appetites are strong in many different ways, are tied to the earth. So, after death, they aren't aware that they have had a transition. In that sense, it's a gradual waking up for them. As to how long, time doesn't exist over there as it does here. It could have been mere seconds to that man who died screaming and yelling; in the earth's account of time it was years.[10]

The soul can remain in the afterlife for years as we count time on earth, before coming to the full realization that death has taken place. Why? Because the change is so very subtle—we've only left the body behind. All that we are as a personality and as a being goes with us. So it behooves all of us to prepare ourselves and assist others as they are preparing to go on that final journey. Hugh Lynn once said that a regular period of meditation isn't just for centering the soul and mind, that it actually builds the body that we will find ourselves in after death!

"Begin to work with meditation," Hugh Lynn said. "Because you can find that Light here—a little dot, a little shaft, a small piece of it—and if you do, you can take it with you. You really can take that with you. And it's a lighted path through [to] the other side."[11]

The doorway we call death is just that—a doorway. We are souls following a magnificent journey through a material world, on a quest to learn to love more fully and deeply and to relinquish our fears and the illusions of our limitations. We are spirit beings, eternal, divine, and endless. As we learn to love ourselves and others more fully, then we can be sure that death will have no sting for us. The love that we realize, manifest, and give to others while on earth will light the path through and beyond this world, beyond the valley of the shadow, to the place in spirit from where we came, the place from where all love and light emanate, the place we call home.

Endnotes

Chapter 1—Edgar Cayce: Discovering the Unseen Worlds
1. Sugrue, Thomas, *There Is a River—The Story of Edgar Cayce* (Virginia Beach, VA: A.R.E. Press, 1973), pp. 56-57.
2. Cayce, Edgar, *What I Believe* (Virginia Beach, VA: A.R.E. Press, 1950), p. 23.
3. Ibid., p. 8.
4. Ibid., p. 9.
5. Sugrue, Thomas, ed., "Editorial," *The New Tomorrow* (December 1929): 3.
6. Ibid., pp. 23-24.
7. Cayce, Hugh Lynn, *God's Other Door* (Virginia Beach, VA: A.R.E. Press, 1958), pp. 12-13.
8. Cayce, E., *What I Believe,* p. 31.
9. Ibid., p. 32.
10. Ibid., pp. 32-33.

Chapter 2—Images of Life After Dying: Near-Death Experiences
1. Moody, Raymond A., M.D., interview by Robert J. Grant, 9/92.
2. Ibid.
3. Moody, Raymond A., M.D., *Life After Life* (Covington, GA: Mockingbird Books, 1975), pp. 23-24.
4. Hudson, Thomson Jay, *The Law of Psychic Phenomena* (Chicago, IL: A.C. McClurg, 1893), p. 310.
5. Ritchie, George, M.D., lecture, Pacific Grove, CA, November 1996.
6. Ritchie, George, M.D., *My Life After Dying* (Charlottesville, VA: Hampton Roads Publishing Co., 1991), p. 15.
7. Ritchie, G., lecture.
8. Ibid.
9. Ibid.
10. Ritchie, George, M.D., with Elizabeth Sherrill, *Return from Tomorrow* (New York, NY: Spire Books, 1978), pp. 49, 52.
11. Ritchie, G., lecture.
12. Ibid.
13. Ibid.

14. Ibid.
15. Ibid.
16. Greaves, H. *Testimony of Light,* pp. 74-75.
17. Ritchie, G., lecture.
18. Ibid.
19. Ibid.
20. Ibid.
21. Ibid.
22. Ibid.
23. Ibid.

Chapter 3—When Death Comes Early or Unexpectedly
1. Gunther, John, *Death Be Not Proud* (New York, NY: HarperCollins, 1989).
2. Bach, Richard, *Illusions—The Adventures of a Reluctant Messiah* (New York, NY: Delacorte Press, 1977), p. 134.
3. Rinpoche, Sogyal, *The Tibetan Book of Living and Dying* (San Francisco, Calif.: HarperSanFrancisco, 1992), p. 183.
4. Pseudonym.
5. Pseudonym.
6. Pseudonym.

Chapter 4—An Account of the Soul's Journey After Death
1. Greaves, Helen, *Testimony of Light* (Essex, England: Neville Spearman Publishers/C.W. Daniel Co., Ltd., 1969), pp. 25-26.
2. Ibid., pp. 17-18.
3. Ibid., pp. 21-22.
4. Ibid., p. 22.
5. Ibid., pp. 23-24.
6. Ibid., pp. 29-30.
7. Ibid., p. 61.
8. Cayce, Hugh Lynn, *The Dimensions of Dying and Rebirth* (Virginia Beach, VA: A.R.E. Press, 1977), pp. 36-37.
9. Greaves, H, *Testimony of Light,* pp. 60-61.
10. Ibid., p. 86.
11. Ibid., pp. 88-89.
12. Ibid., pp. 93-95.

13. Ibid., p. 96.
14. Ibid., p. 61.
15. Ibid., p. 62.
16. Ibid., pp. 63-64.

Chapter 5—*Reassurances from Beyond*
1. Cayce, Edgar Evans, private interview by Robert J. Grant, 6/96.
2. Cayce, Hugh Lynn, "The First Ten Minutes After Death," taped lecture, 1976.
3. Ibid.
4. Ibid.
5. Ibid.
6. Ibid.
7. Ibid.
8. Ibid.
9. Ibid.
10. Ibid.
11. Ibid.
12. Ibid.
13. Ibid.

Chapter 6—*Case Studies of After-Death Communication*
1. Greaves, H, *Testimony of Light*, pp. 77-78.
2. Ibid, pp. 78-79.
3. Ibid., pp. 79-80.
4. Cayce, H. L., *Dimensions of Dying and Rebirth*, p. 32.
5. Ibid., pp. 32-33.
6. Ibid., p. 33.
7. Pseudonym. Jay is a twenty-one-year-old man in the U.S. Navy who lives in Virginia.
8. Private interview by Robert J. Grant, June 1998.
9. Ibid.
10. Hudson, Thomson J., *The Law of Psychic Phenomena* (Chicago, IL: A.C. McClurg & Co. Publishers, 1893), p. 296.
11. Ibid., pp. 295-296.
12. Pseudonym. Barbara is a sixty-four-year-old nurse who lives in Ohio.

13. Private interview by Robert J. Grant, July 1997.
14. Pseudonym. Janet is a forty-five-year-old homemaker who lives in Ohio.
15. Private interview with Robert J. Grant, August 1998.
16. Grant, Robert J., article, "Assurances from a Departed Loved One," *A.R.E. Community* (April 1993): 2.
17. Pseudonym. Bob is a thirty-eight-year-old researcher who lives in Virginia.
18. Private interview by Robert J. Grant, April 1995.
19. Pseudonym. Susan is a forty-one-year-old landscape designer who lives in Virginia.
20. Private interview by Robert J. Grant, May 1998.
21. Ibid.
22. Pseudonym. Heather is a thirty-four-year-old homemaker who lives in Virginia.
23. Private interview by Robert J. Grant, November 1998.
24. Moody, R., interview.
25. Ibid.
26. Ibid.
27. Ibid.
28. Ibid.
29. Moody, Raymond, M.D., with Paul Perry, *Reunions—Visionary Encounters with Departed Loved Ones* (New York, NY: Villard Books, 1993), pp. 206-208.

Chapter 7—Spirit Communication:
A Bridge Between Here and Hereafter
1. Cayce, H.L, *God's Other Door*, pp. 10-11.
2. Ibid., pp. 21-22.
3. Roberts, Jane, *Seth Speaks: The Eternal Validity of the Soul* (New York: Prentice-Hall Press, 1972), p. ix.
4. Ibid., p. x.
5. *The Seth Video* (New York, NY: Kendall Enterprises, Inc., 1986).
6. Ibid.
7. Roberts, J., *Seth Speaks*, pp. 17-18.
8. Roberts, Jane, *The Seth Material* (Englewood Cliffs, NJ: Prentice-Hall Press, Inc., 1970), pp. 64-66.

9. Ibid., p. 74.
10. *The Seth Video.*
11. Roberts, Jane, *The Afterdeath Journal of an American Philosopher—The Worldview of William James* (Englewood Cliffs, NJ: Prentice Hall Press, Inc., 1977), p. 3.
12. Ibid., pp. 7-11.
13. Ibid., pp. 13-14.
14. Ibid., p. 23.
15. Ibid., pp. 19-23.
16. Windsor, James, Ph.D., interview by Robert J. Grant, April 1988.
17. Roberts, J., *The Afterdeath Journal of an American Philosopher*, pp. 120-121.
18. Ibid., p. 123.
19. Dorothy Rohrbach is a certified hypnotherapist and founder of the Center for Harmonic Vibrational Therapy®, Inc., in Southfield, Michigan.
20. Rohrbach, Dorothy, interview by Robert J. Grant, November 1998.
21. Ritchie, G., *Return from Tomorrow*, p. 124.

Chapter 8—The Shadowlands: Earthbound Souls and Hell
1. Pseudonym.
2. Reports of reading 827-1.
3. Ibid.
4. Ritchie, G., lecture.
5. Cayce, Hugh Lynn, "Dimensions of Death," panel discussion, Virginia Beach, Virginia, 1976.
6. Ritchie, G. *Return from Tomorrow,* p. 61.
7. Ibid., pp. 63-64.
8. Ritchie, G., lecture.
9. Ibid.
10. Ibid.
11. Pearce-Higgins, J.D., ed., *Life, Death, and Psychical Research,* Chapter 10, "Poltergeists, Hauntings, and Possession" (London, England: Rider and Company, 1973), pp. 176-177.
12. Cayce, H.L., lecture.
13. Ritchie, G., lecture.

14. Ibid.
15. Ibid.
16. Ibid.
17. Ibid.
18. Greaves, H. *Testimony of Light,* pp. 96-98.
19. Scott, Cyril, *The Boy Who Saw True* (Essex, England: Neville Spearman Publishers/C.W. Daniel Co., Ltd., 1953), pp. 105-106.
20. Ibid., p. 106.
21. Ibid., pp. 108-111.
22. Cayce, H.L., interview 11/81.

Chapter 9—Preparing for Life in the Next World
1. Cayce, H.L., "Dimensions of Death," panel discussion.
2. Cayce, H.L., *Dimensions of Dying and Rebirth,* pp. 65-66.
3. Rinpoche, Sogyal, *The Tibetan Book of Living and Dying* (San Francisco, Calif.: HarperSanFrancisco, 1992), p. 108.
4. Ibid., p. 59.
5. Ibid., p. 60.
6. *Study Group Readings,* The Edgar Cayce Library Series, Vol. 7 (Virginia Beach, Va: A.R.E. Press, 1977).
7. Cayce, H.L., interview.
8. Rinpoche, S., *The Tibetan Book of Living and Dying,* pp. 20-21.
9. Ibid., pp. 22-23.
10. Cayce, H.L., lecture.
11. Ibid.

Selected Bibliography

Bach Richard. *Illusions—The Adventures of a Reluctant Messiah.* New York, NY: Delacorte Press, 1977.

Bailey, Alice. *Death: The Great Adventure.* New York, NY: Lucis Publishing Co., 1985.

Bucke, Richard Maurice. *Cosmic Consciousness—A Study in the Evolution of the Human Mind.* New York, NY: E.P. Dutton and Company, Inc., 1901.

Butts, Robert. *The Seth Video.* New York, NY: Kendall Enterprises, 1986.

Cayce Edgar. *Life and Death—Volume One.* The Edgar Cayce Library Series, Virginia Beach, VA: A.R.E. Press, 1973.

———. *The Continuity of Life.* Virginia Beach, VA: A.R.E. Press, 1958.

———. *What I Believe.* Virginia Beach, VA: A.R.E. Press, 1950.

Cayce Hugh Lynn. *Dimensions of Dying and Rebirth.* Virginia Beach, VA: A.R.E. Press, 1977.

———. *God's Other Door.* Virginia Beach, VA: A.R.E. Press, 1958.

———. *Venture Inward—Edgar Cayce's Story and the Mysteries of the Unconscious Mind.* Virginia Beach, VA: A.R.E. Press, 1964.

Ford, Arthur, as told to Jerome Ellison. *The Life Beyond Death.* New York, NY: G.P. Putnam's Sons, 1971.

Frejer, Ernest B., *The Edgar Cayce Companion.* Virginia Beach, VA: A.R.E. Press, 1995.

Grant, Robert J., *Are We Listening to the Angels?—The Next Step in Understanding Angels in our Lives.* Virginia Beach, VA: A.R.E. Press, 1994.

———. *Love & Roses from David—A Legacy of Living and Dying.* Virginia Beach, VA: A.R.E. Press, 1994.

Greaves, Helen. *Testimony of Light.* Essex, England: Neville Spearman Publishers/C.W. Daniel Co., Ltd., 1969.

Gunther, John. *Death Be Not Proud.* New York, NY: Harper-Collins, 1989.

Gurney, Edmund; Myers, F.W.H.; Podmore, Frank. *Phantasms of the Living.* London, England: Kegan Paul, Trench, Trubner & Co., Ltd., 1918.

Hudson, Thomson Jay. *The Law of Psychic Phenomena.* Chicago, IL: A.C. McClurg & Co., 1893.

Leadbeater, C.W. *The Inner Life: Volume I.* Wheaton, IL: The Theosophical Press, 1942.

Lodge, Sir Oliver J. *Raymond or Life and Death.* New York, NY: George H. Doran Company, 1916.

Maeterlinck, Maurice. *Our Eternity.* New York, NY: Dodd, Mead, and Company, 1913.

Moody, Raymond A., M.D., *Life After Life—The Investigation of a Phenomenon—Survival of Bodily Death.* Covington, GA: Mockingbird Books, 1975.

Moody, Raymond A., M.D., with Paul Perry. *Reunions—Visionary Encounters with Departed Loved Ones.* New York, NY: Villard Books, 1993.

Morse, Melvin. *Closer to the Light—Learning from the Near-*

Death Experiences of Children. New York: Ivy Books, 1990.

Ouspensky, P.D. *Tertium Organum—The Third Canon of Thought: A Key to the Enigmas of the World.* New York, NY: Alfred A Knopf, 1964.

Pearce-Higgins, J.D., ed. *Life, Death and Psychical Research.* London: Rider and Company, 1973.

Prabhavananda, Swami, trans., Isherwood, Christopher. *The Bhagavad-Gita.* Hollywood, CA: The Marcell Rodd Co., 1944.

Rinpoche, Sogyal. *The Tibetan Book of Living and Dying.* San Francisco, CA: HarperSanFrancisco, 1992.

Ritchie, George G., M.D. *My Life After Dying.* Charlottesville, VA: Hampton Roads Publishing, 1991.

Ritchie, George, M.D., with Elizabeth Sherrill. *Return from Tomorrow.* Tarrytown, NJ: Baker Book House/Spire Books, 1978.

Roberts, Jane. *The Seth Material.* Englewood Cliffs, NJ: Prentice-Hall, 1970.

———. *Seth Speaks—The Eternal Validity of the Soul.* Englewood Cliffs, NJ: Prentice-Hall, 1972.

———. *The Afterdeath Journal of an American Philosopher— The World View of William James.* Englewood Cliffs, NJ: Prentice-Hall, 1978.

Scott, Cyril. *The Boy Who Saw True.* Essex, England: Neville Spearman Publishers/C.W. Daniel Co., Ltd., 1953.

Sechrist, Elsie R. *Death Does Not Part Us.* Virginia Beach, VA: A.R.E. Press, 1992.

Smith, Robert A. *About My Father's Business—The Amazing Story of Hugh Lynn Cayce.* Norfolk, VA: Donning & Company, 1988.

Sparrow, G.S. *Lucid Dreaming—Dawning of the Clear Light.* Virginia Beach, VA: Blue Mantle Press, 1999.

Sugrue, Thomas J. *There Is a River—The Story of Edgar Cayce.* Virginia Beach, VA: A.R.E. Press, 1973.

White, Stuart Edward. *The Unobstructed Universe.* New York, NY: E.P. Dutton & Company, Inc., 1940.

Wickland, Carl A. *Thirty Years Among the Dead.* London, England: Spiritualist Press, 1924.